Gymnastics COLORING BOOK

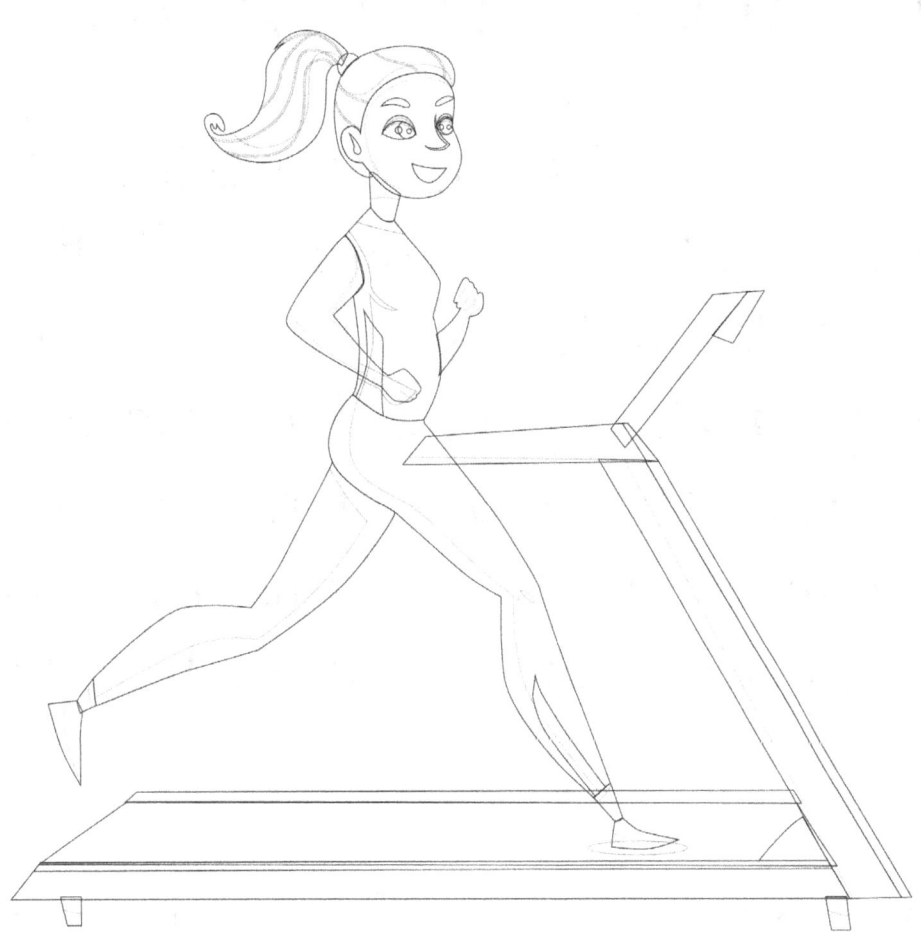

This book belong to:

....

Thank you for purchasing this quality coloring book from Nicholas Nicky!

Inside this book are 50 unique and fun gymnastics coloring pages designed especially for Girls.

Each image is on its own page with a BLANK backside to help avoid color bleed-through if you color with markers or other ink based pens. If you use something other than colored pencils or crayons, we also recom-mend placing a sheet of paper or some other blotter between your coloring page and the one beneath it while you work.

We hope you enjoy your Gymnastics Coloring Book!

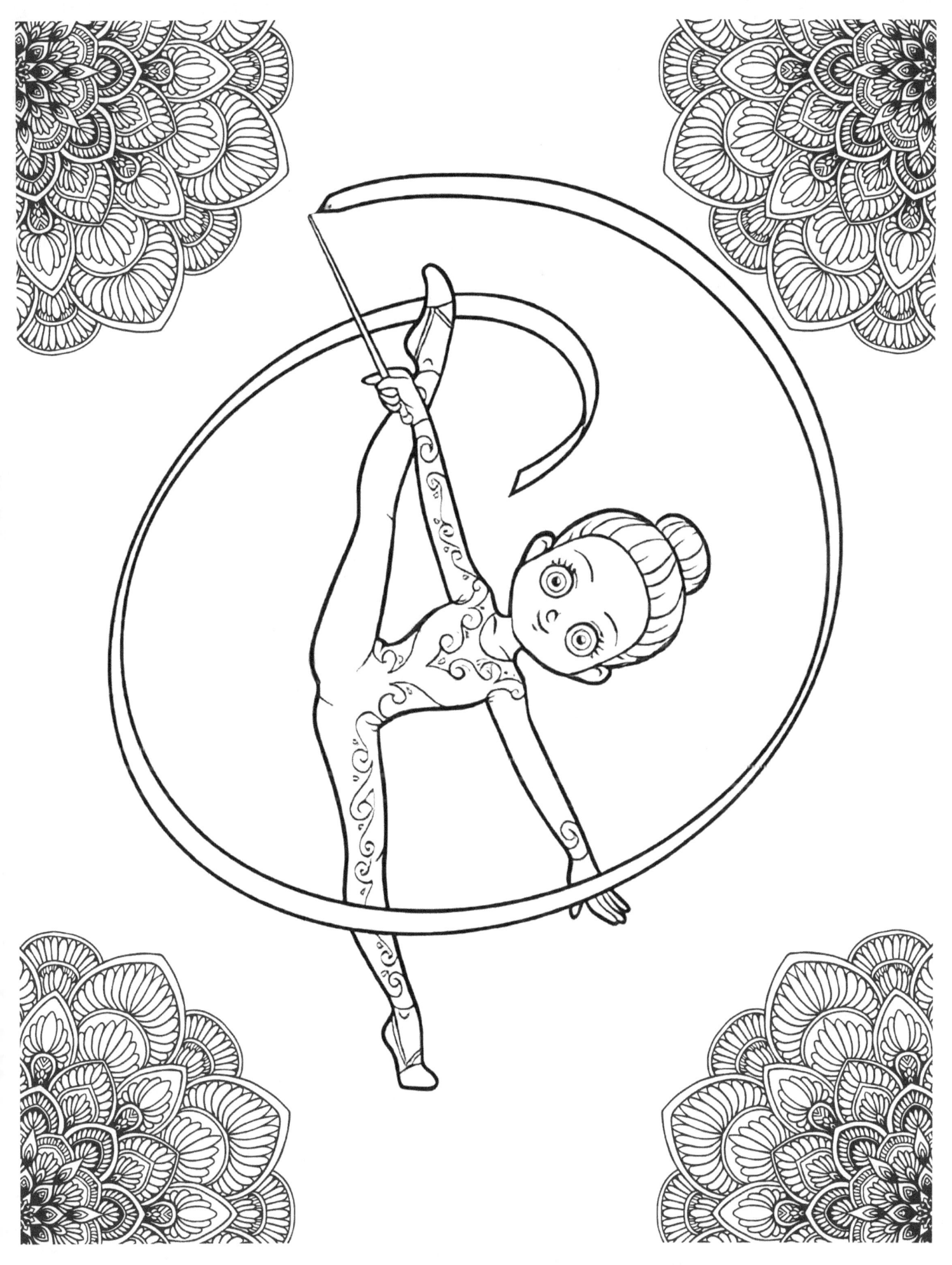

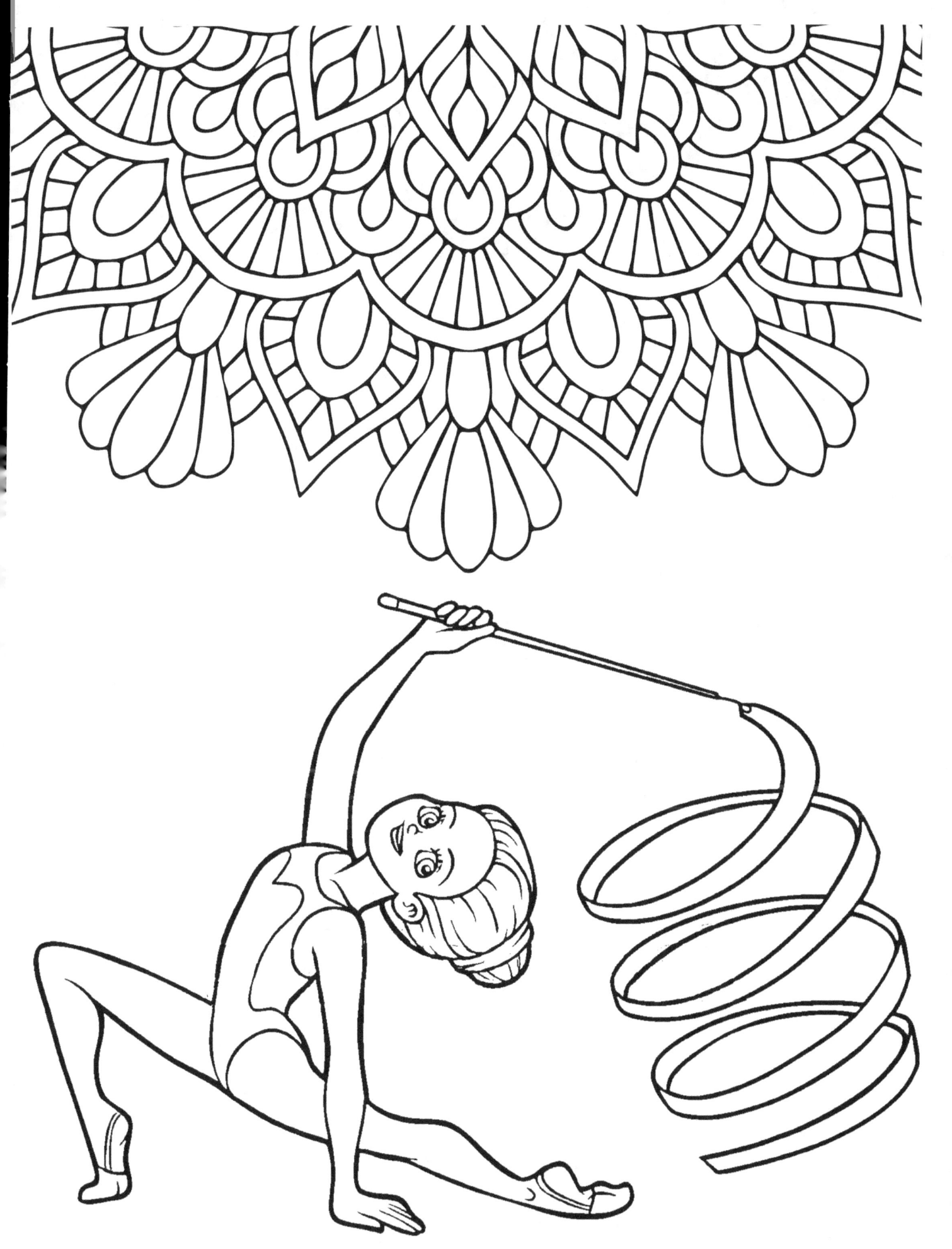

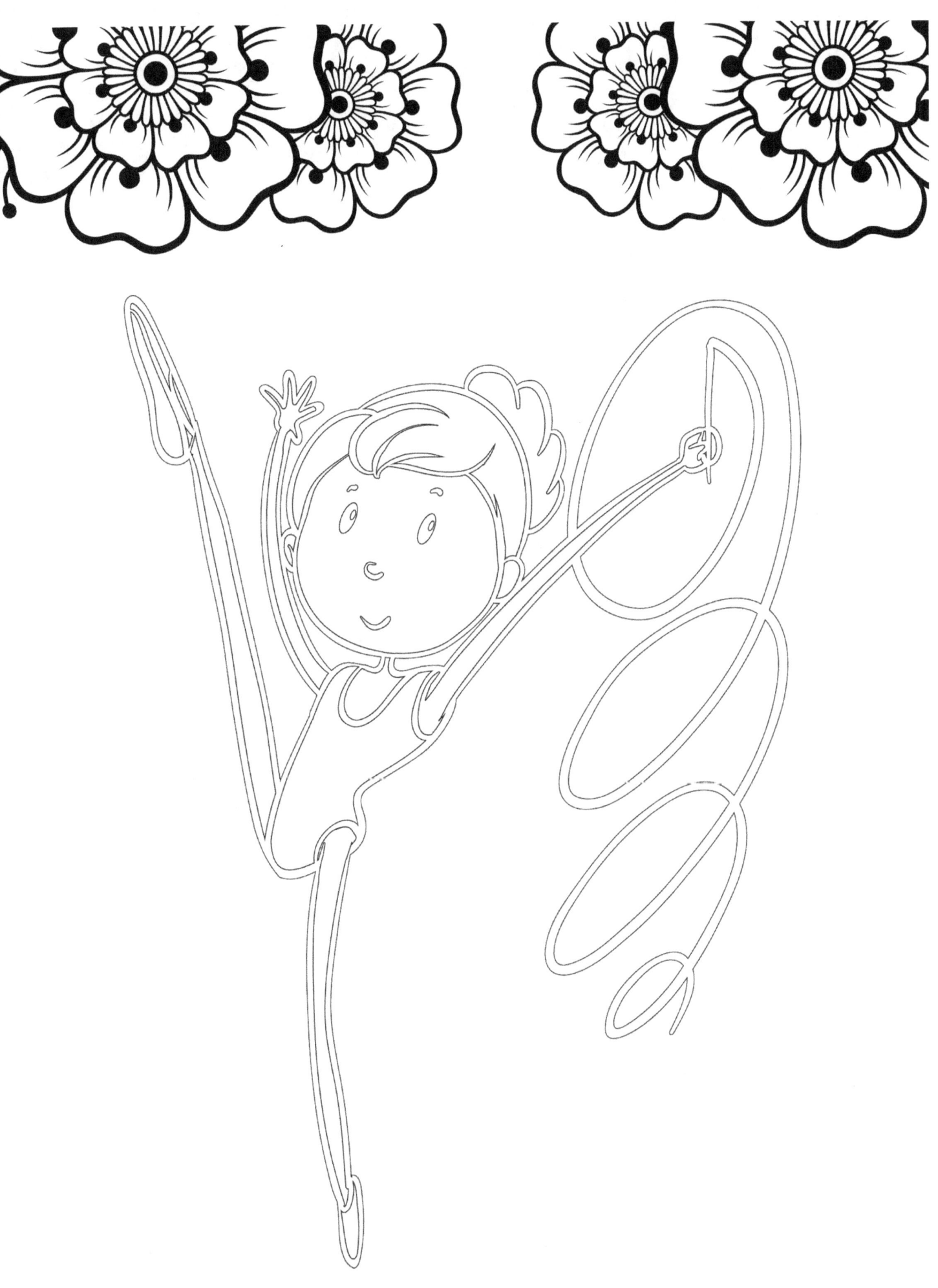

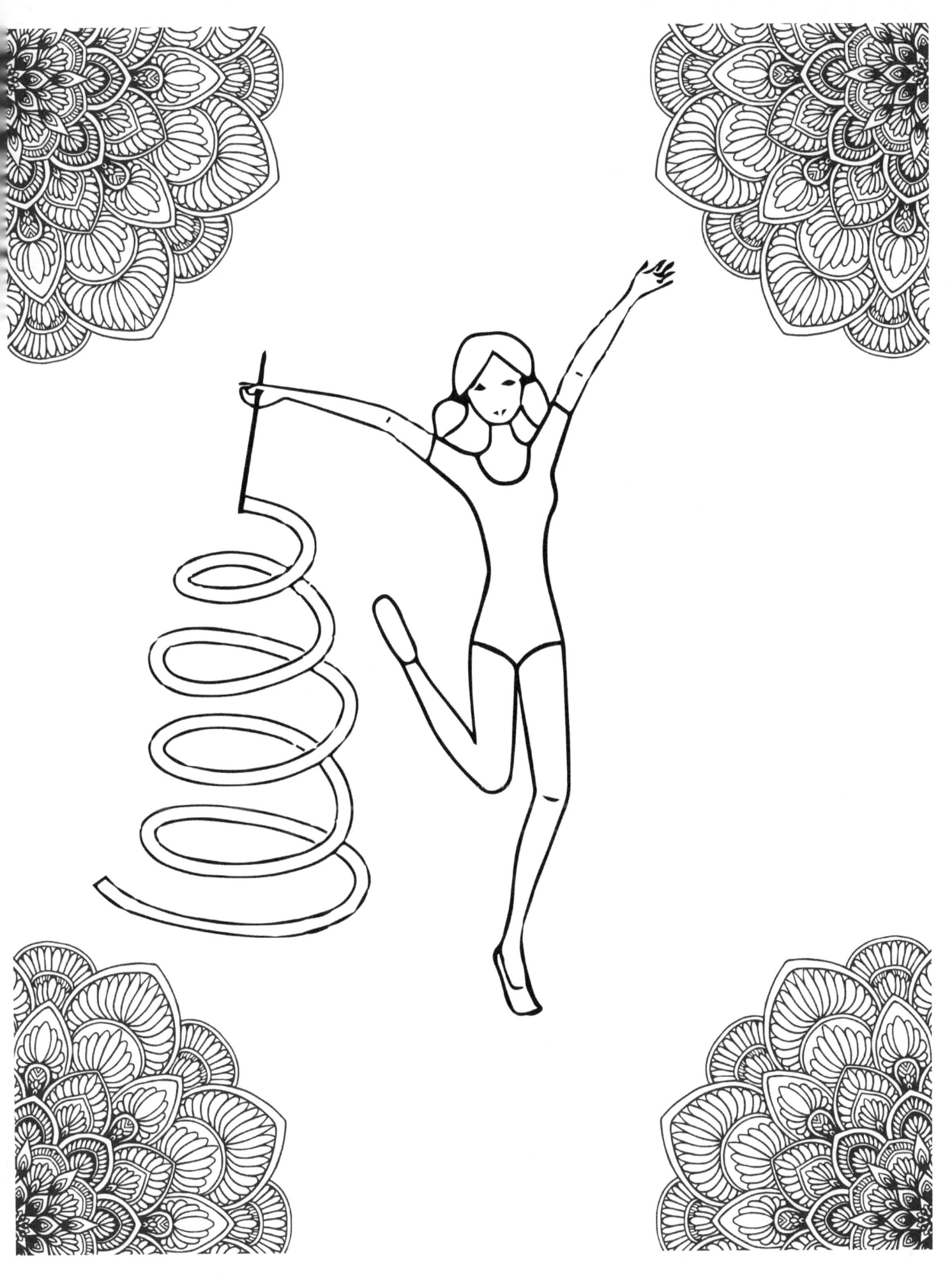

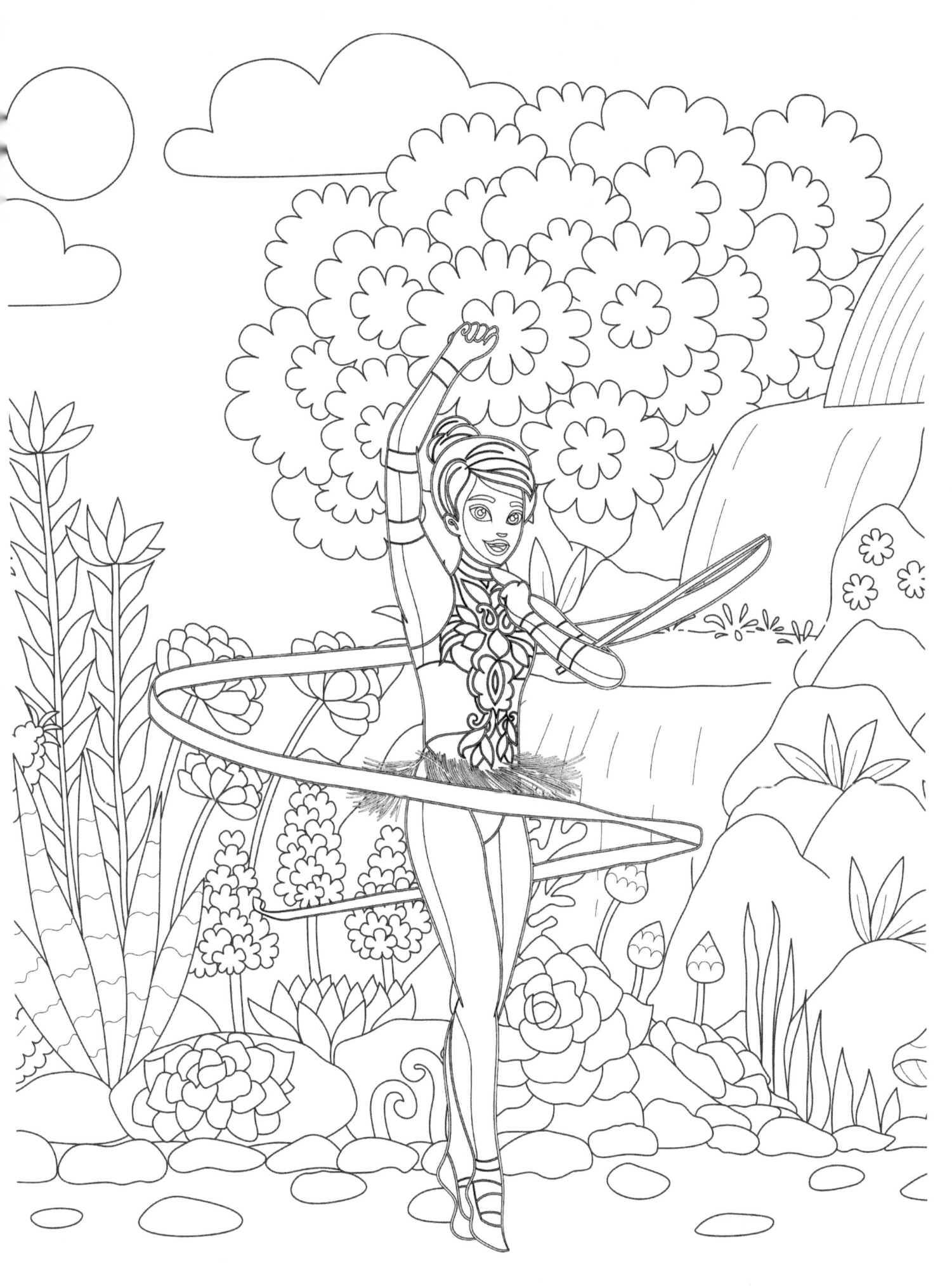

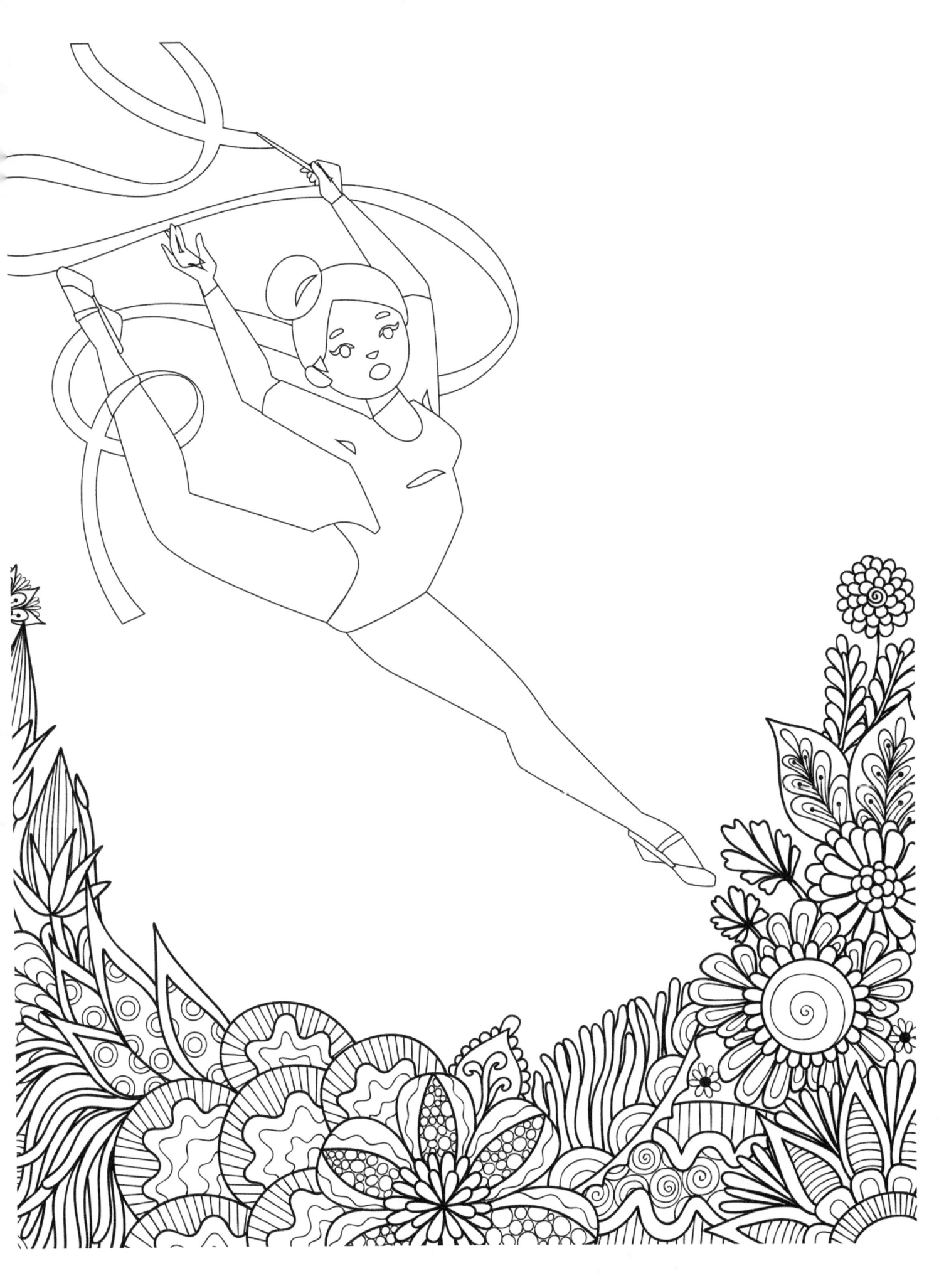

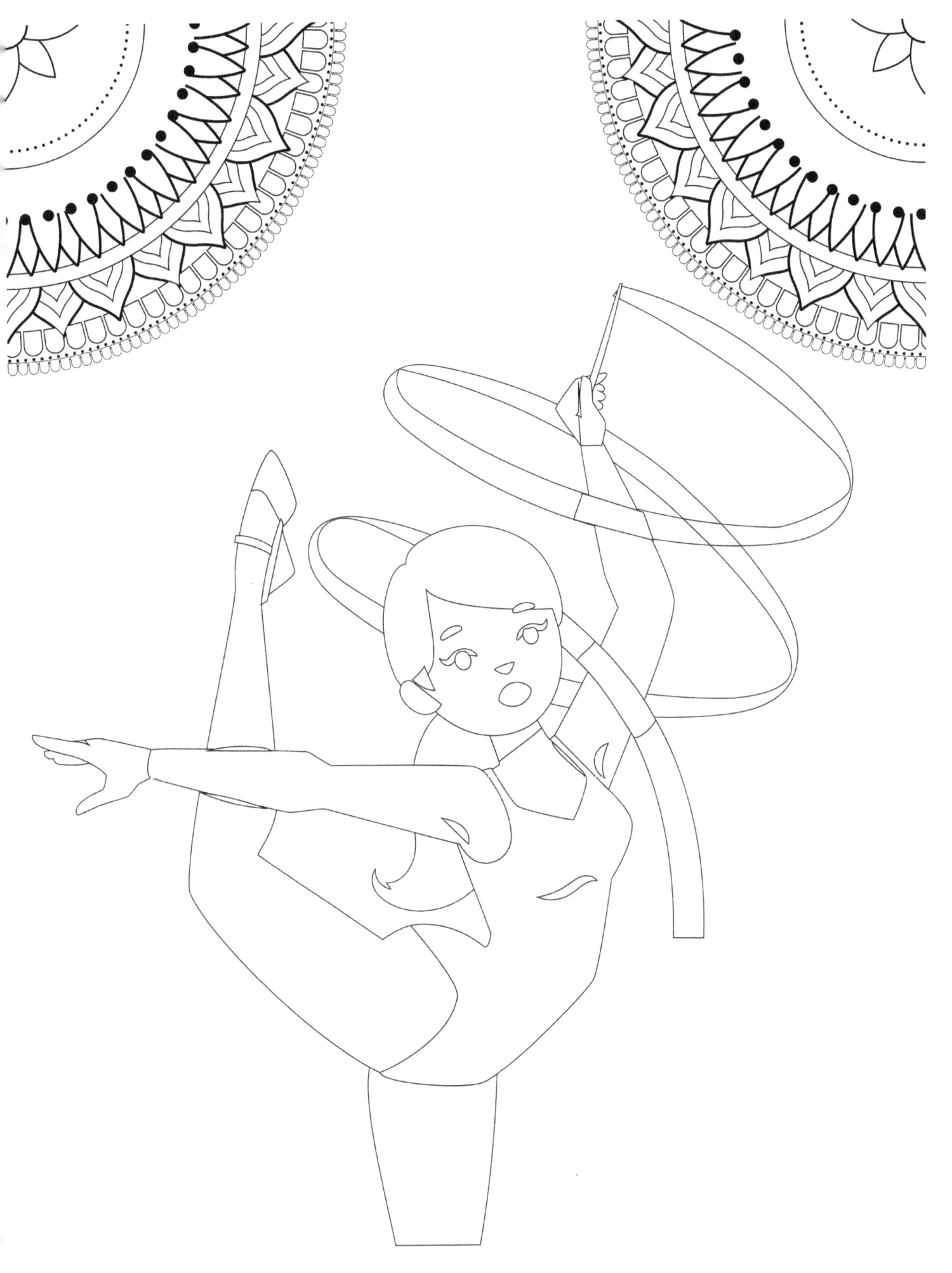

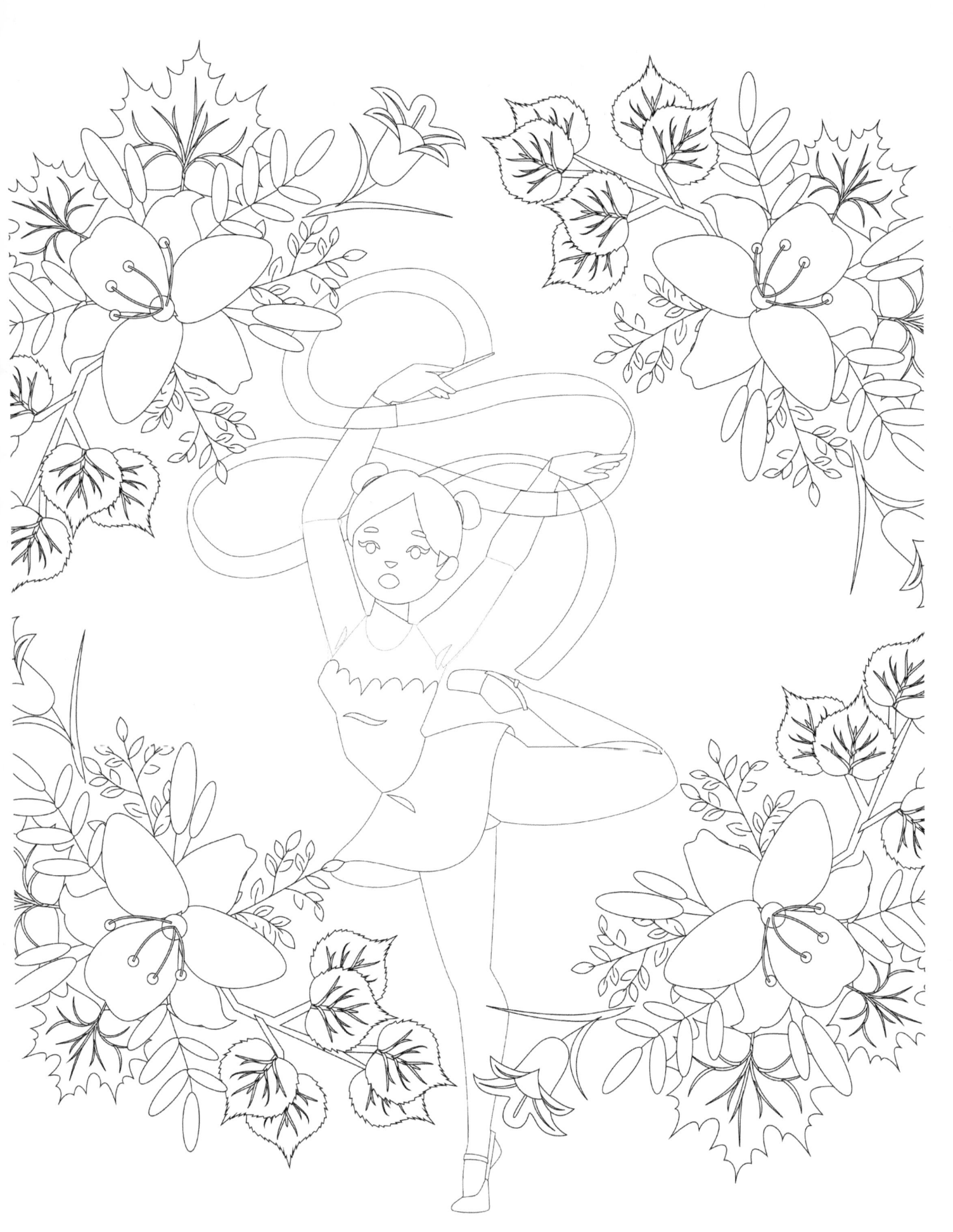

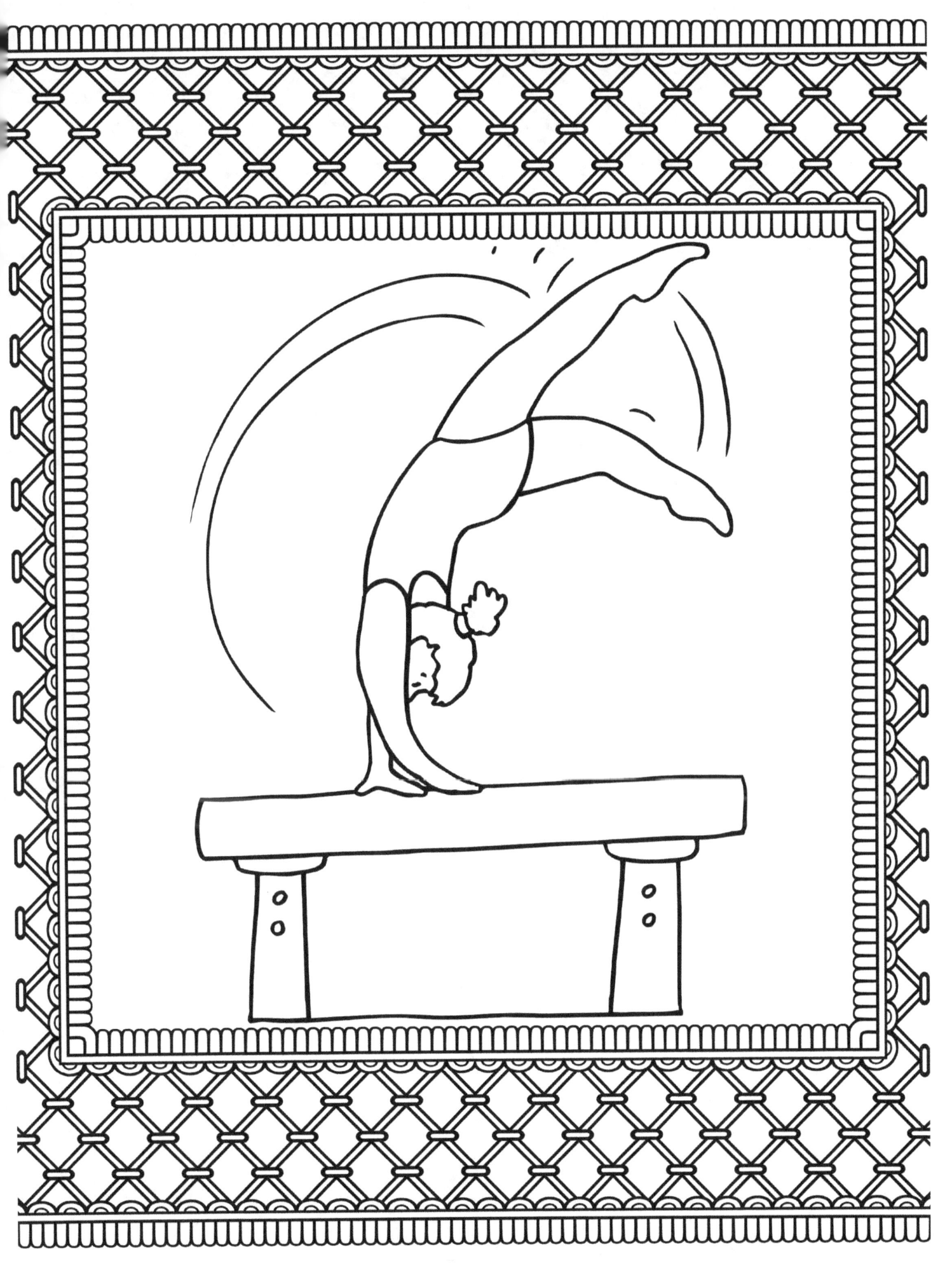

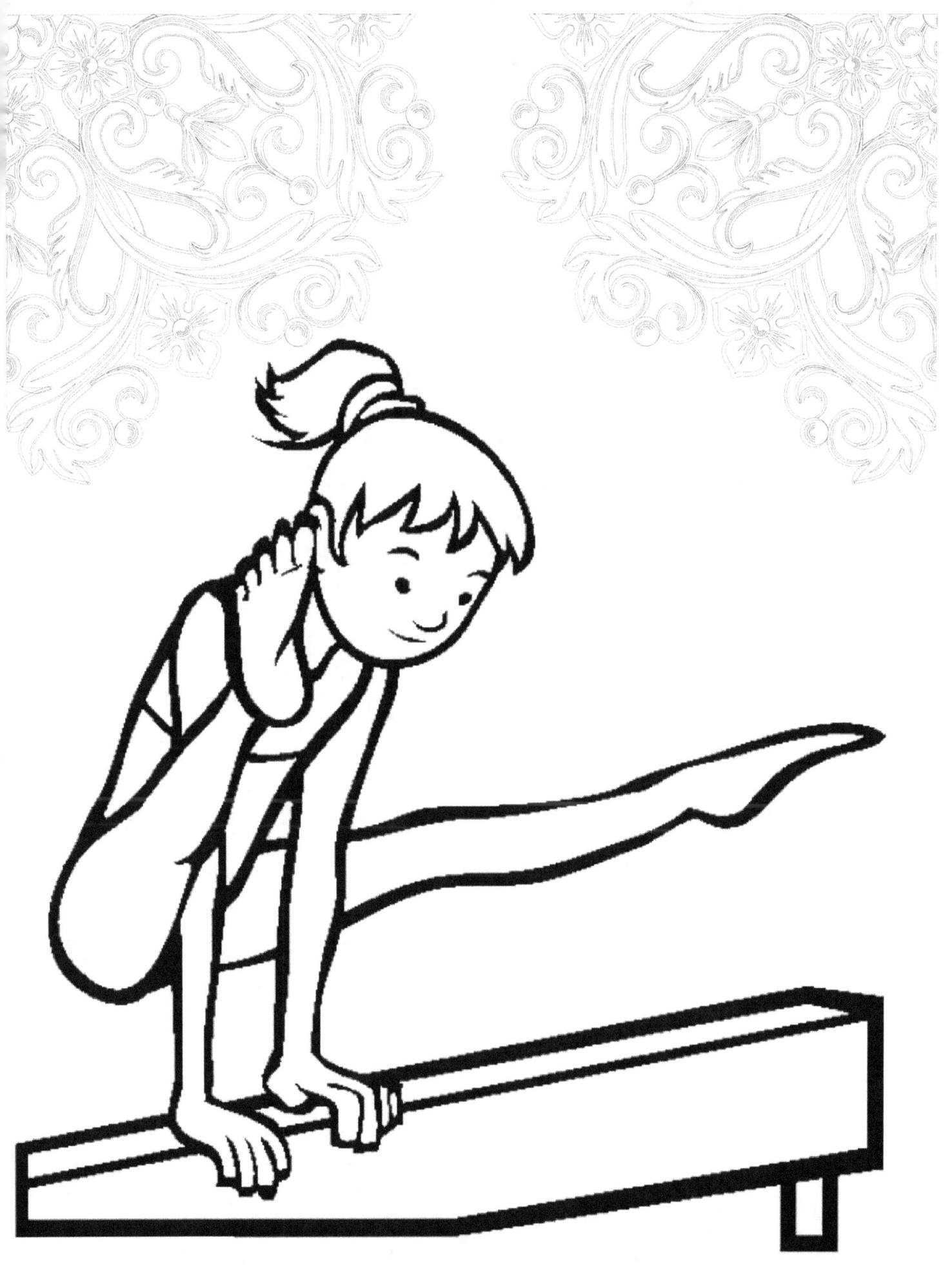

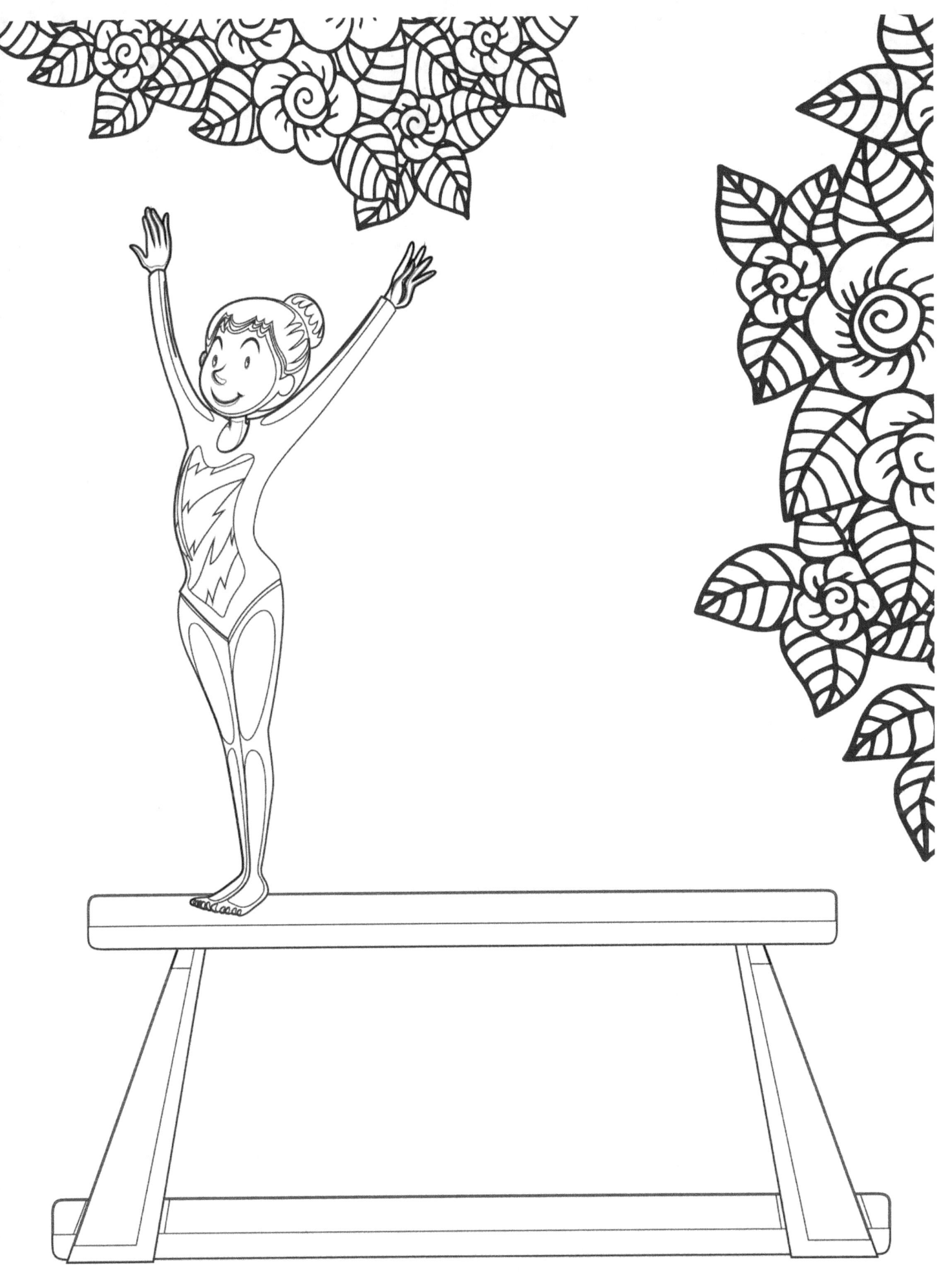

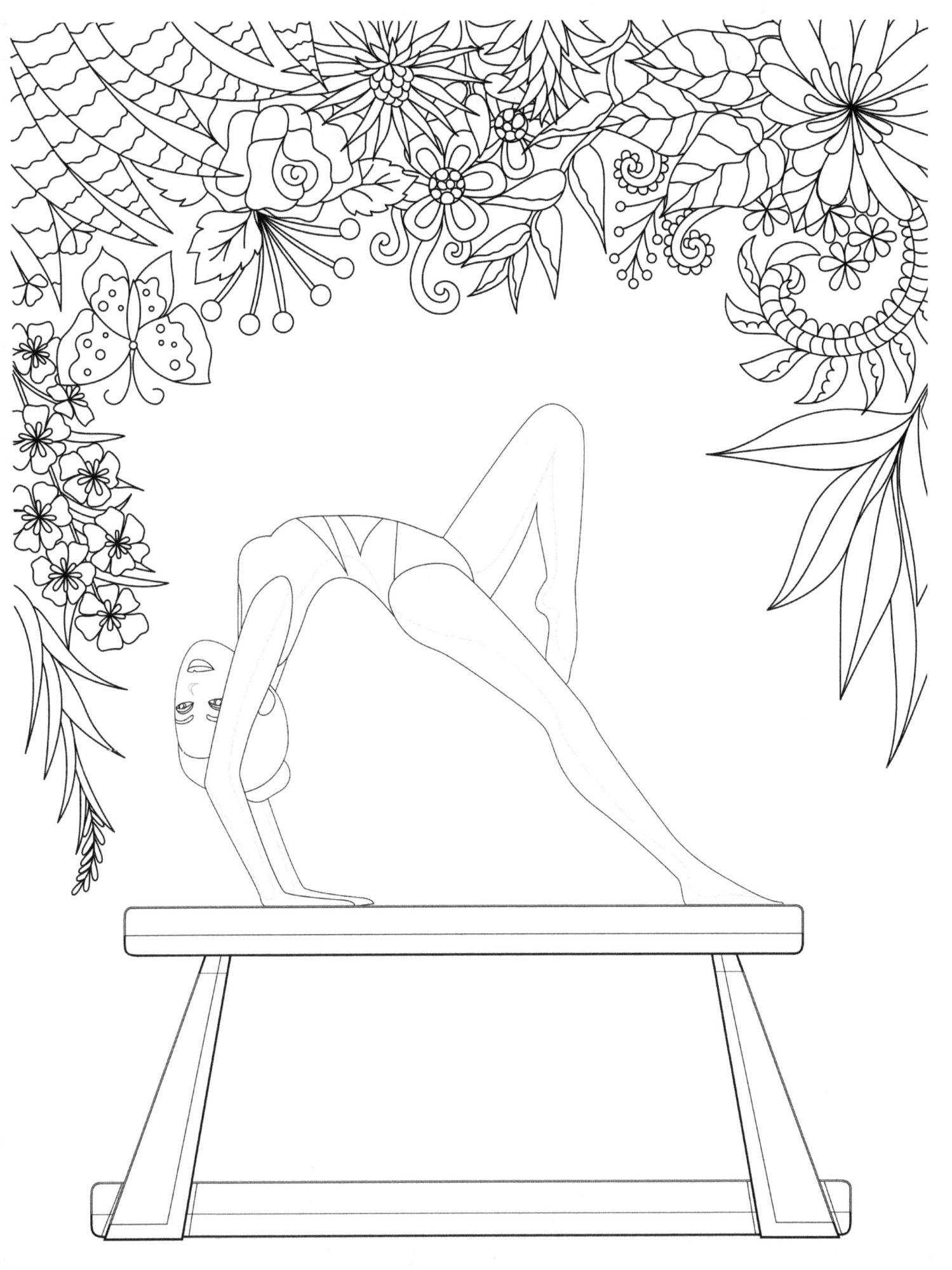

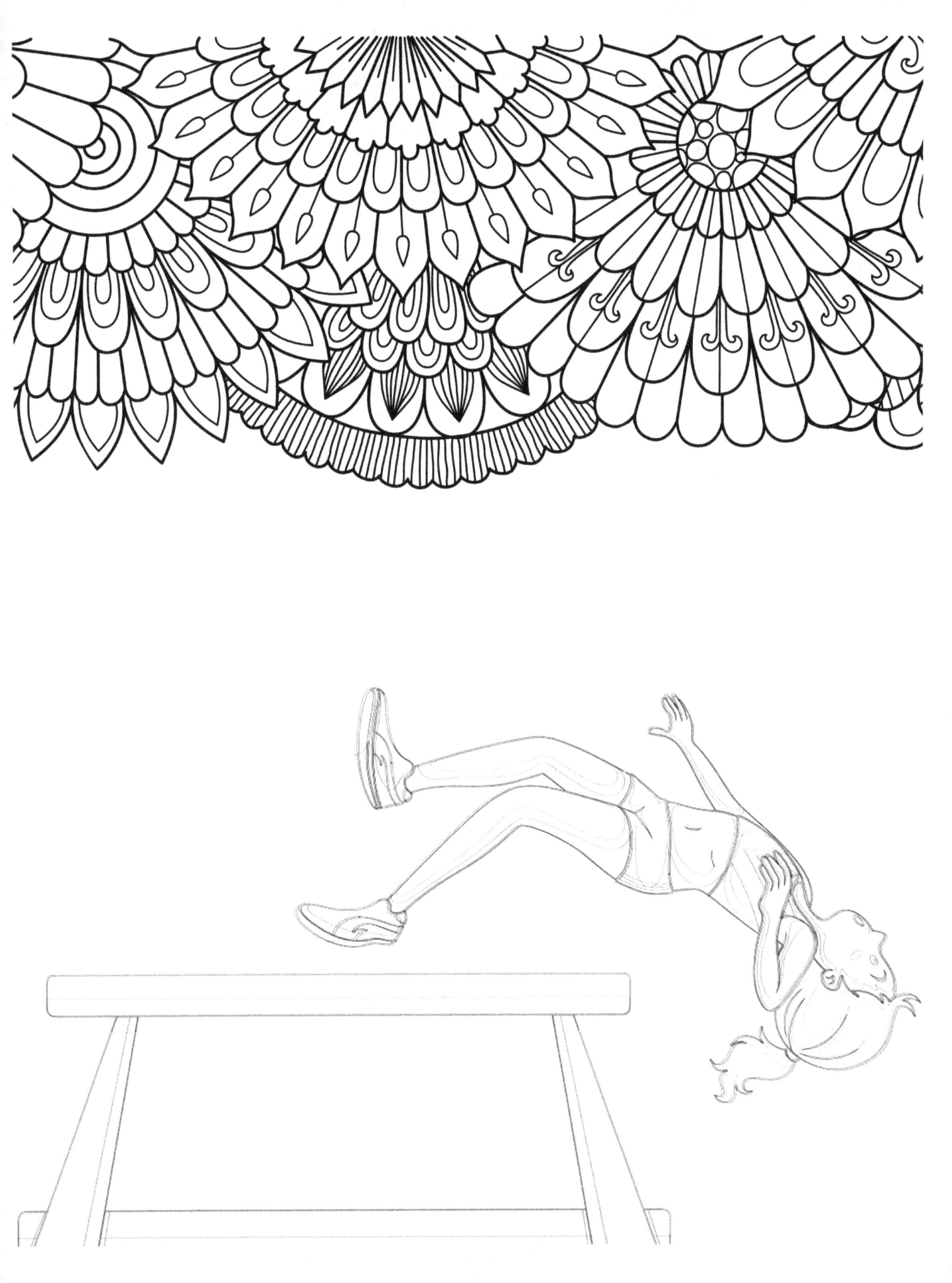

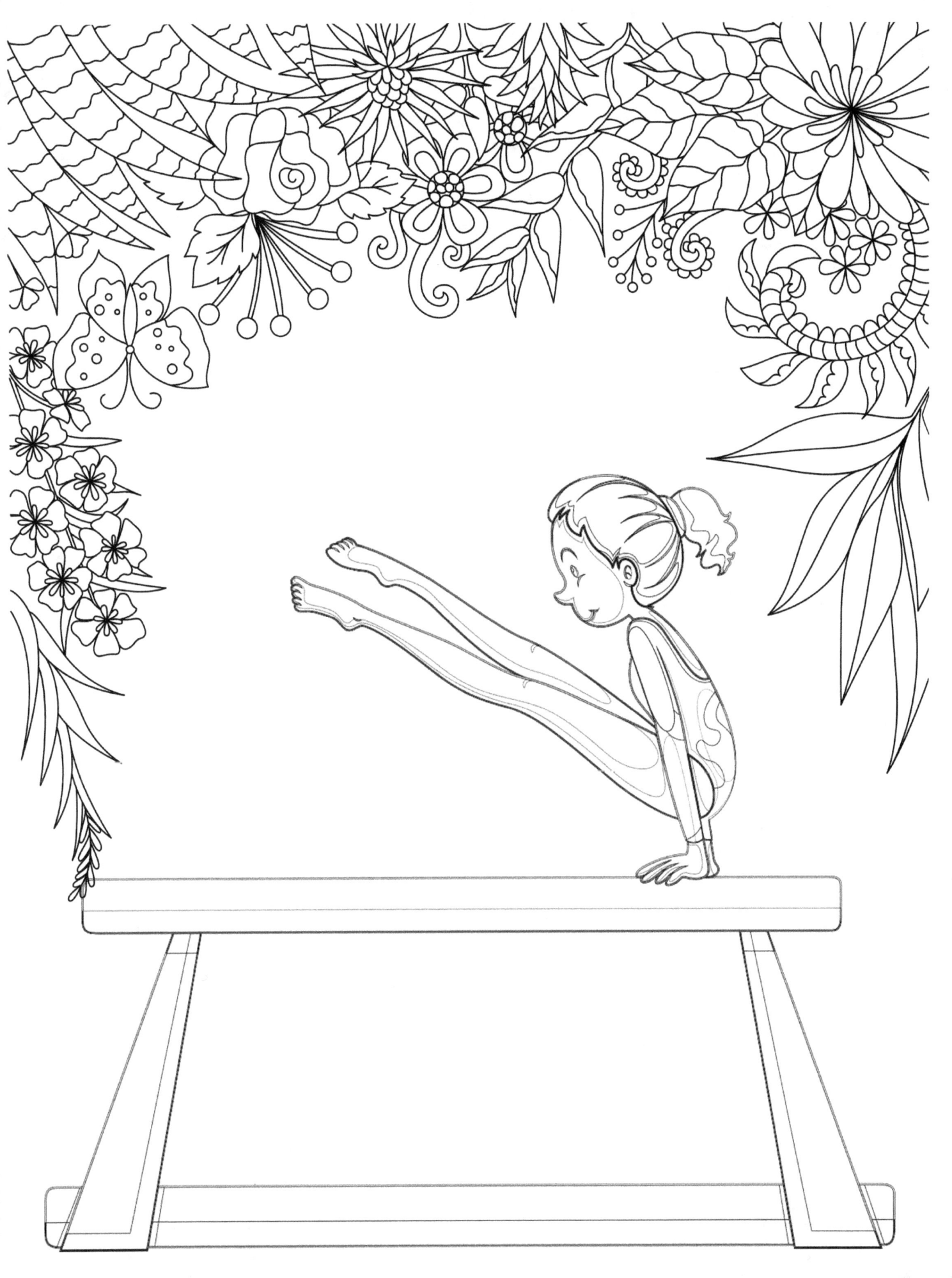

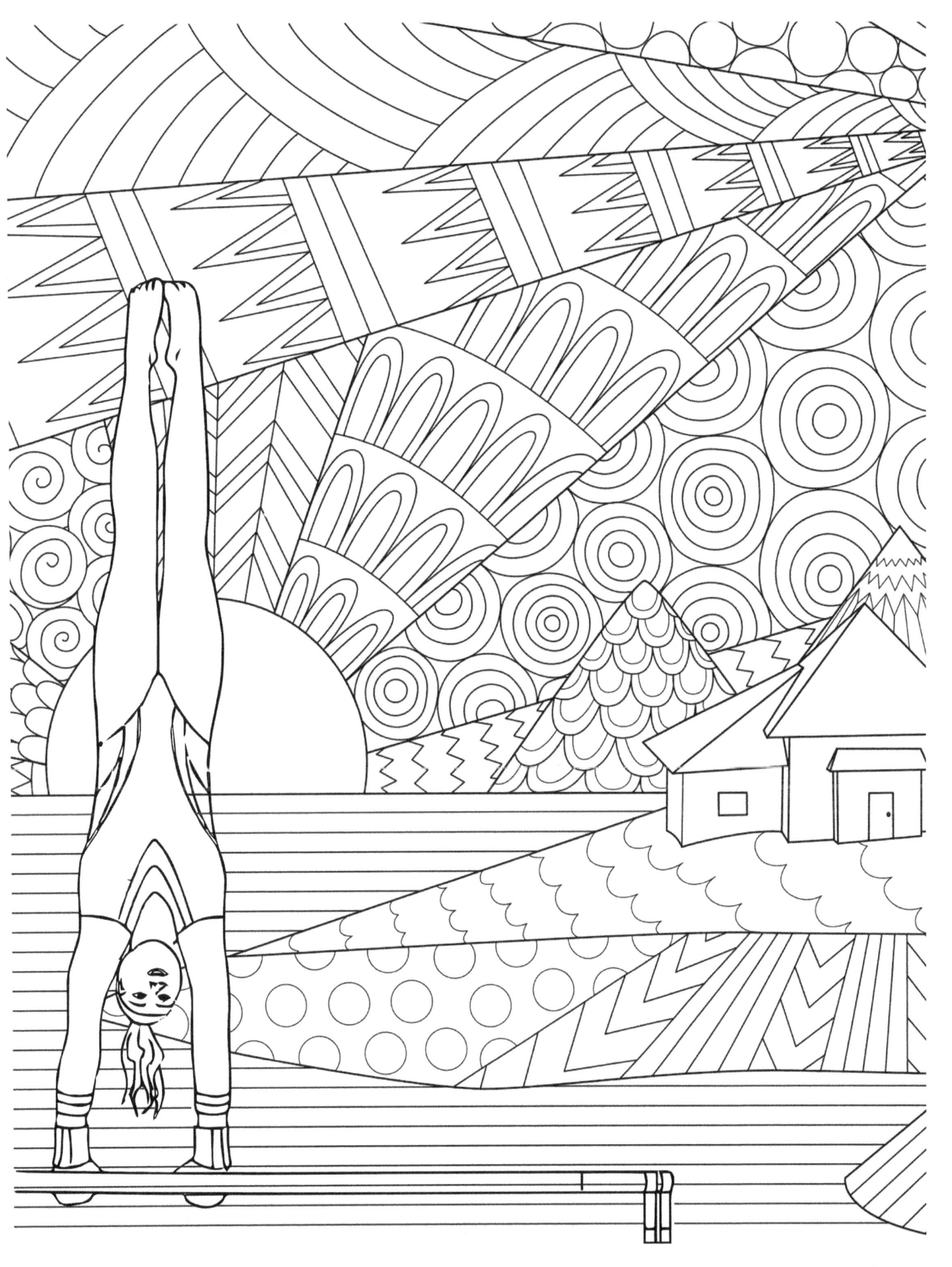

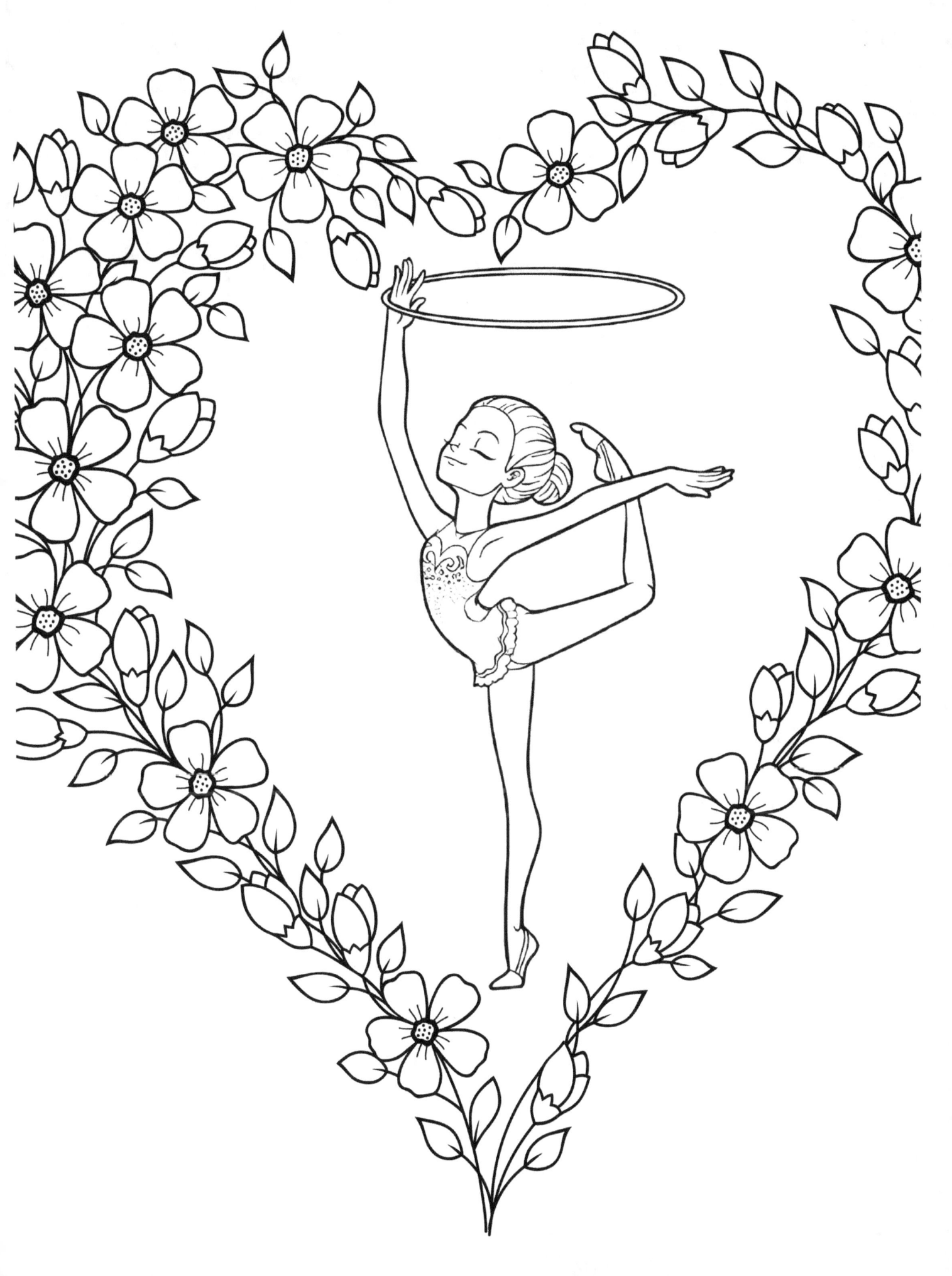

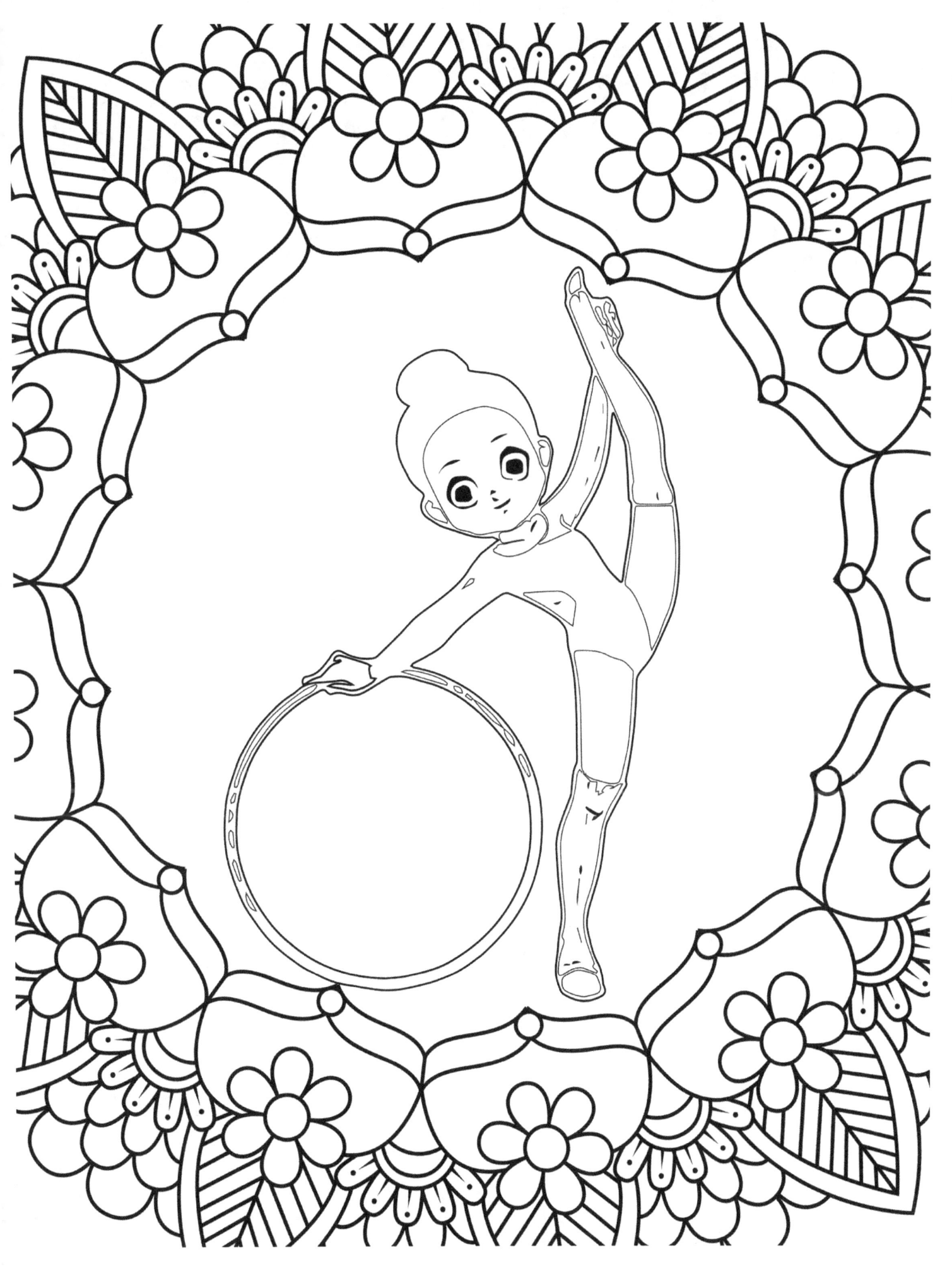

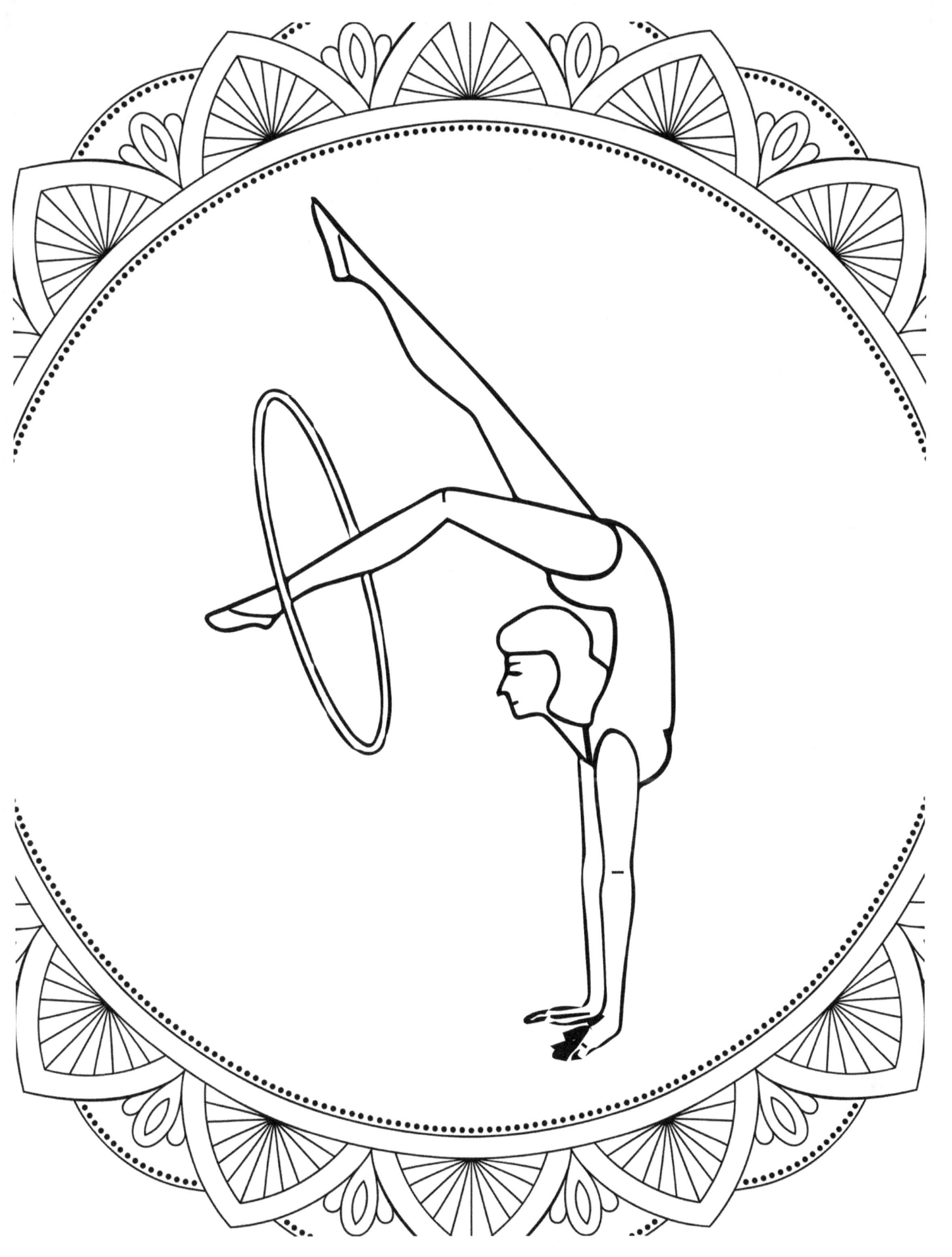

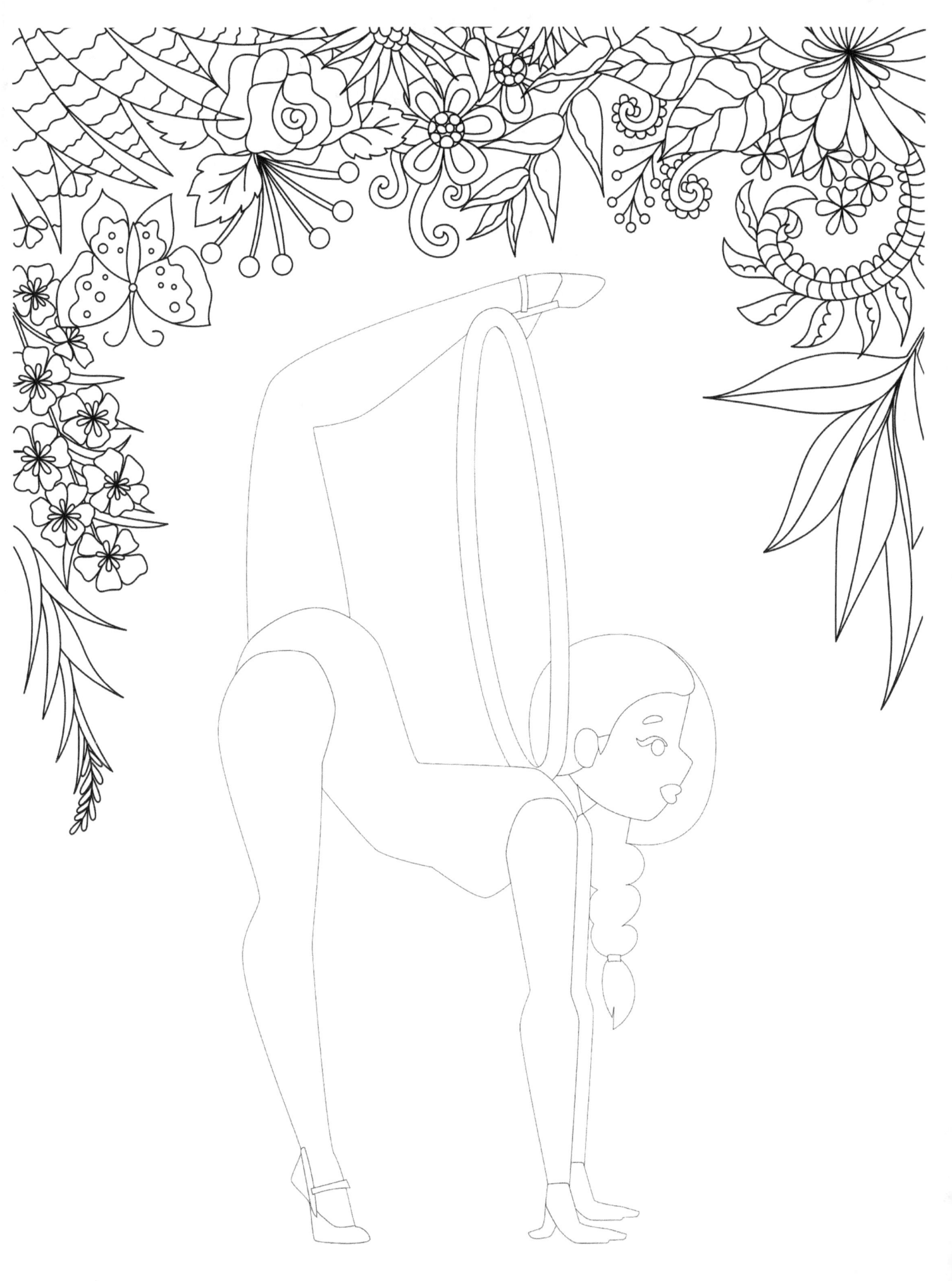

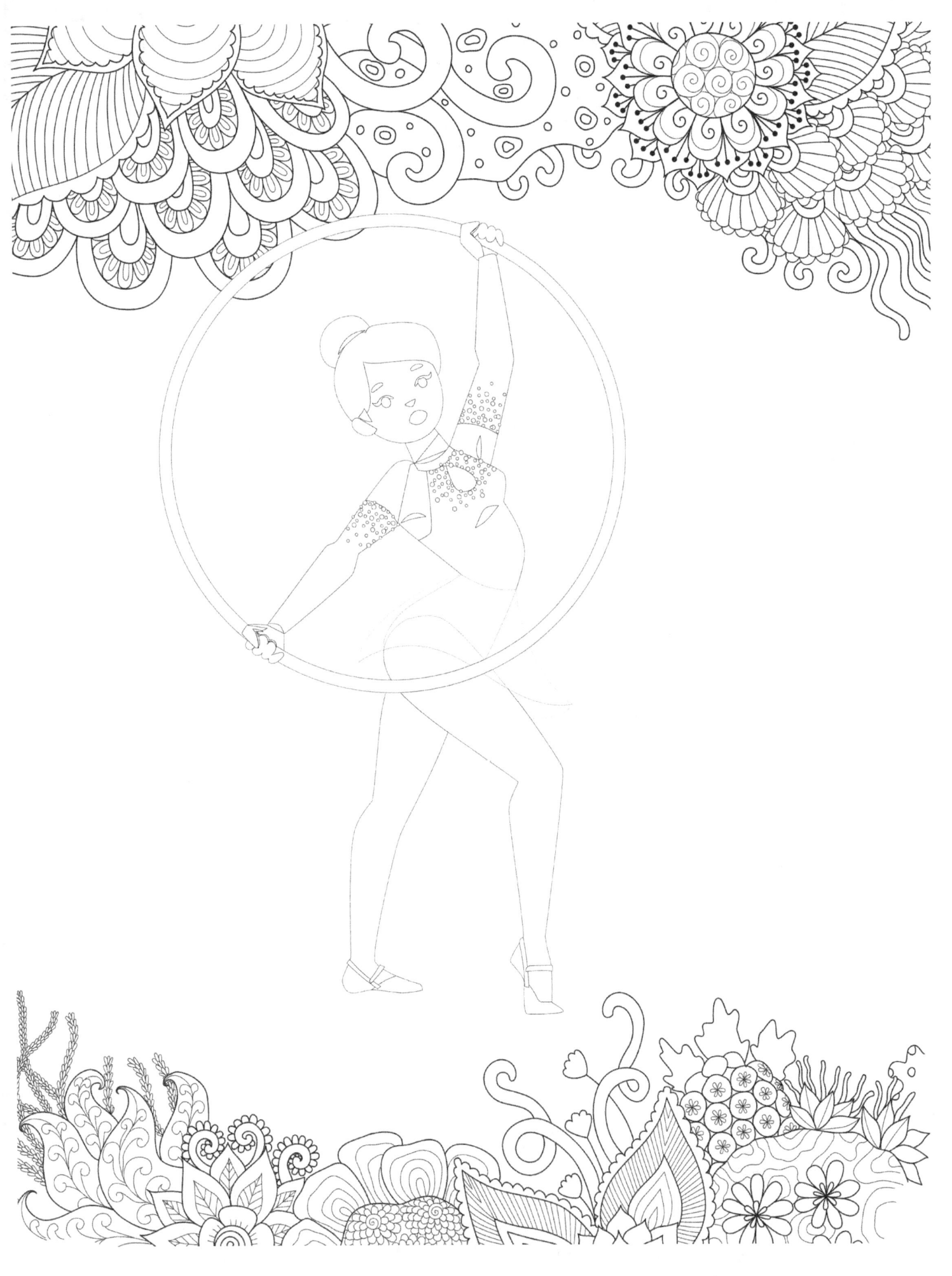

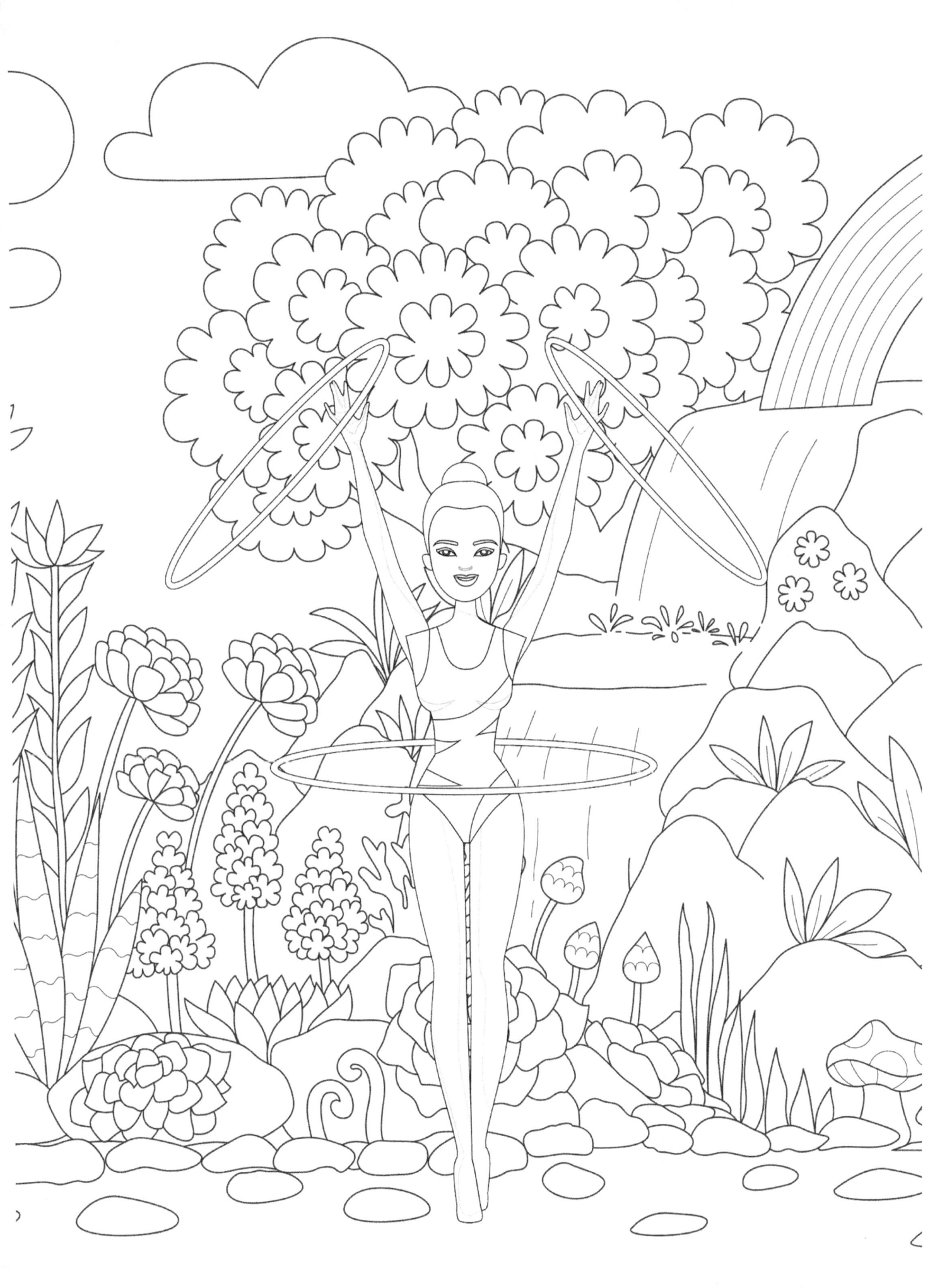

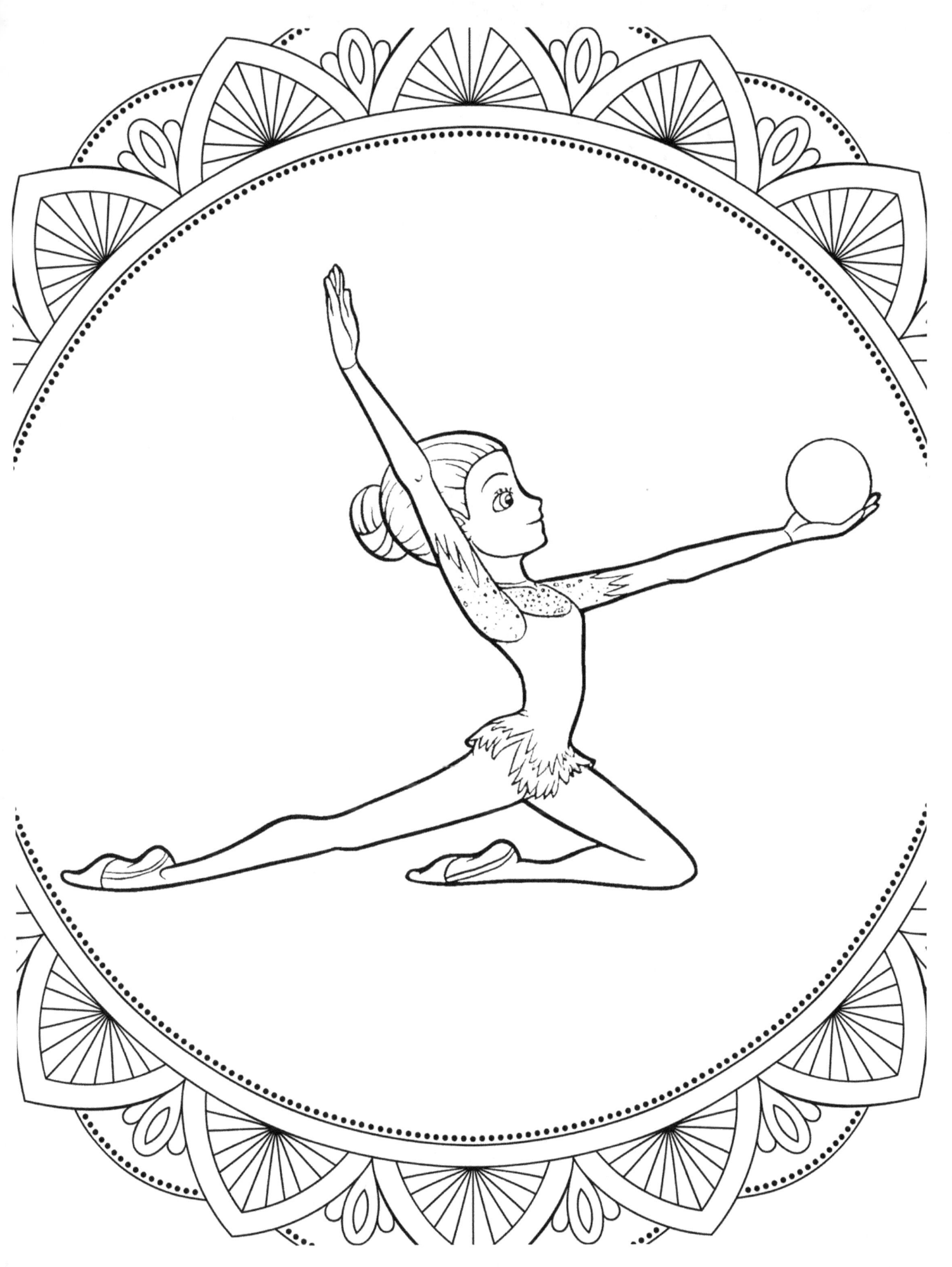

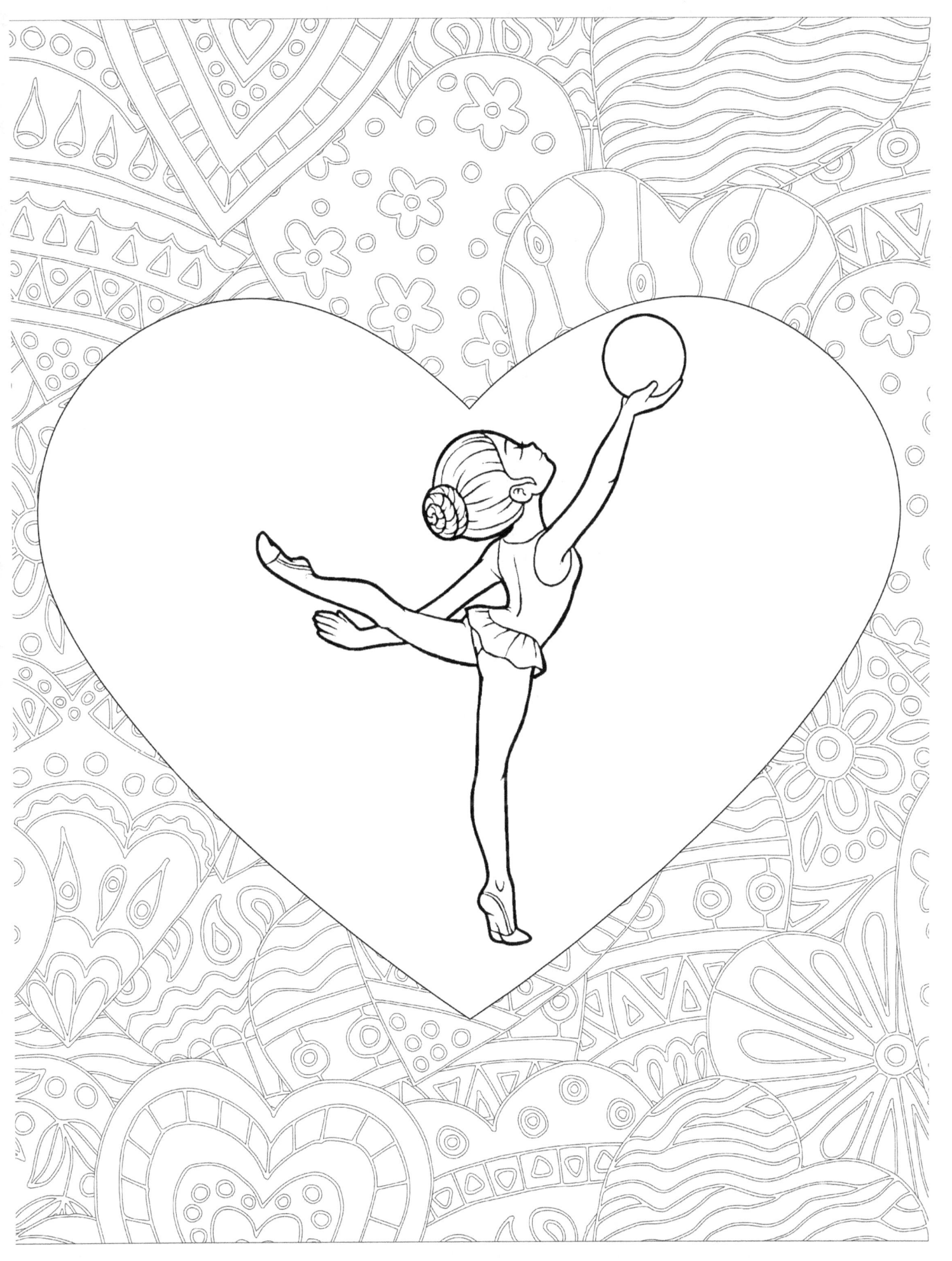

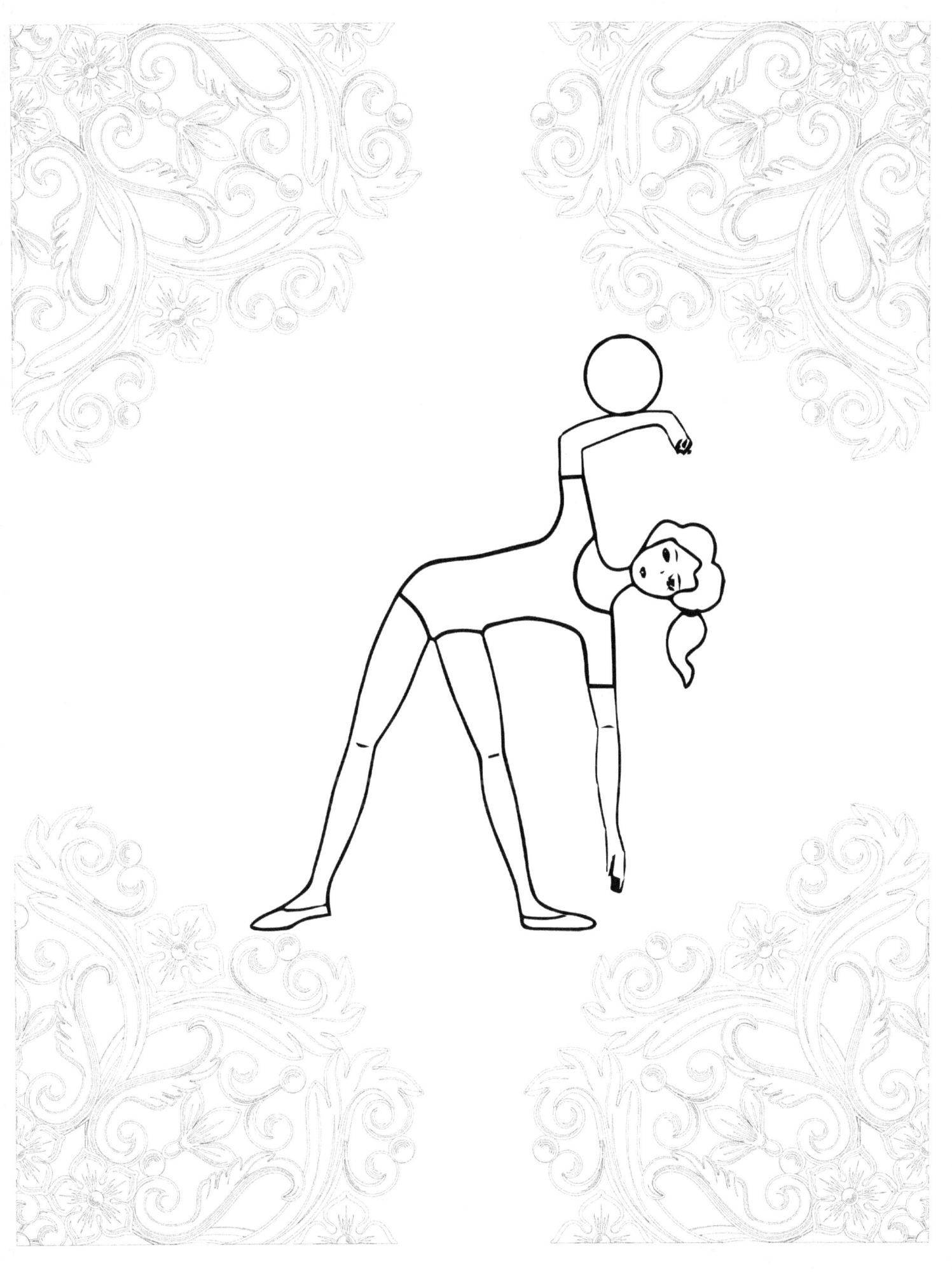

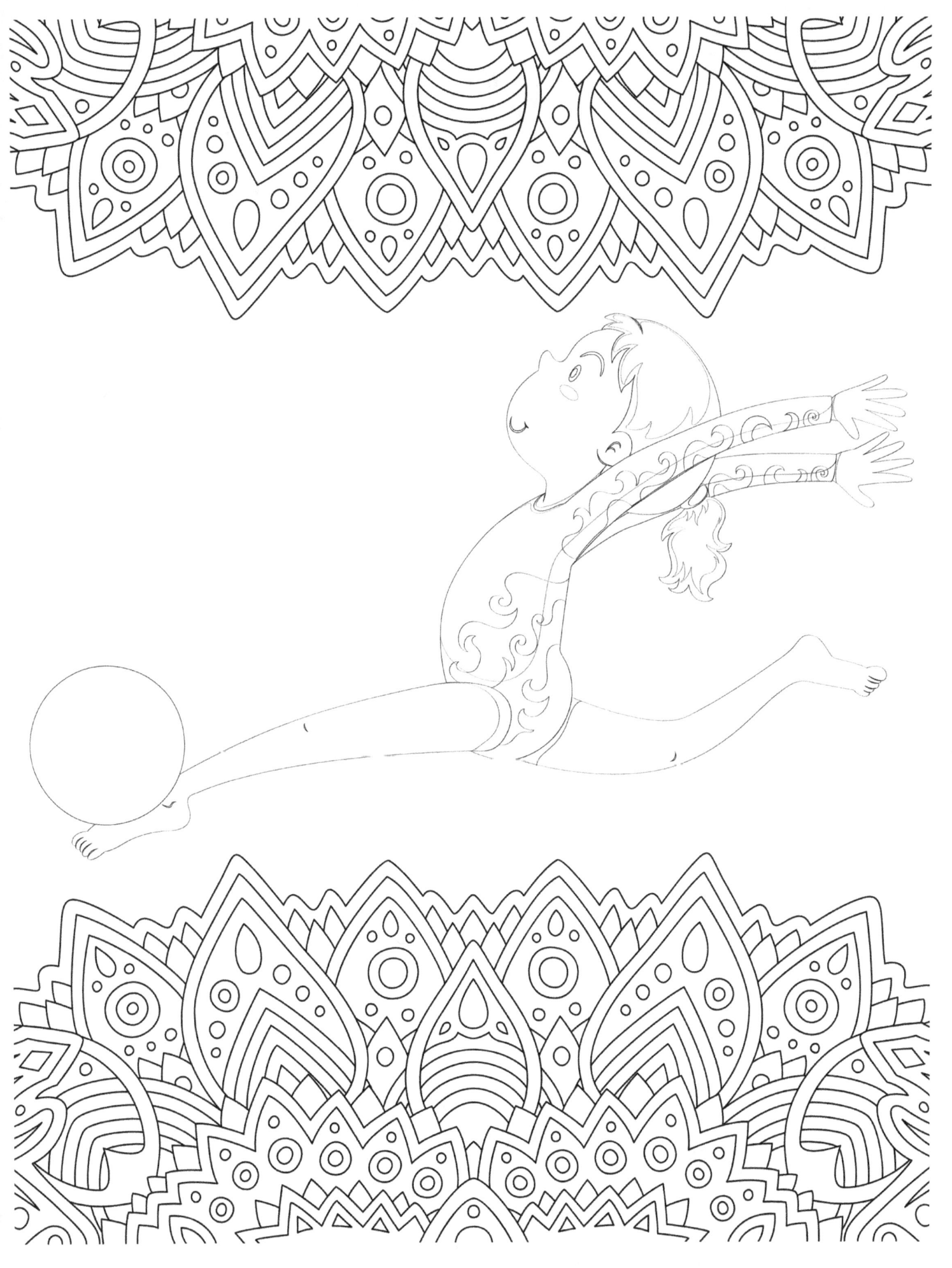

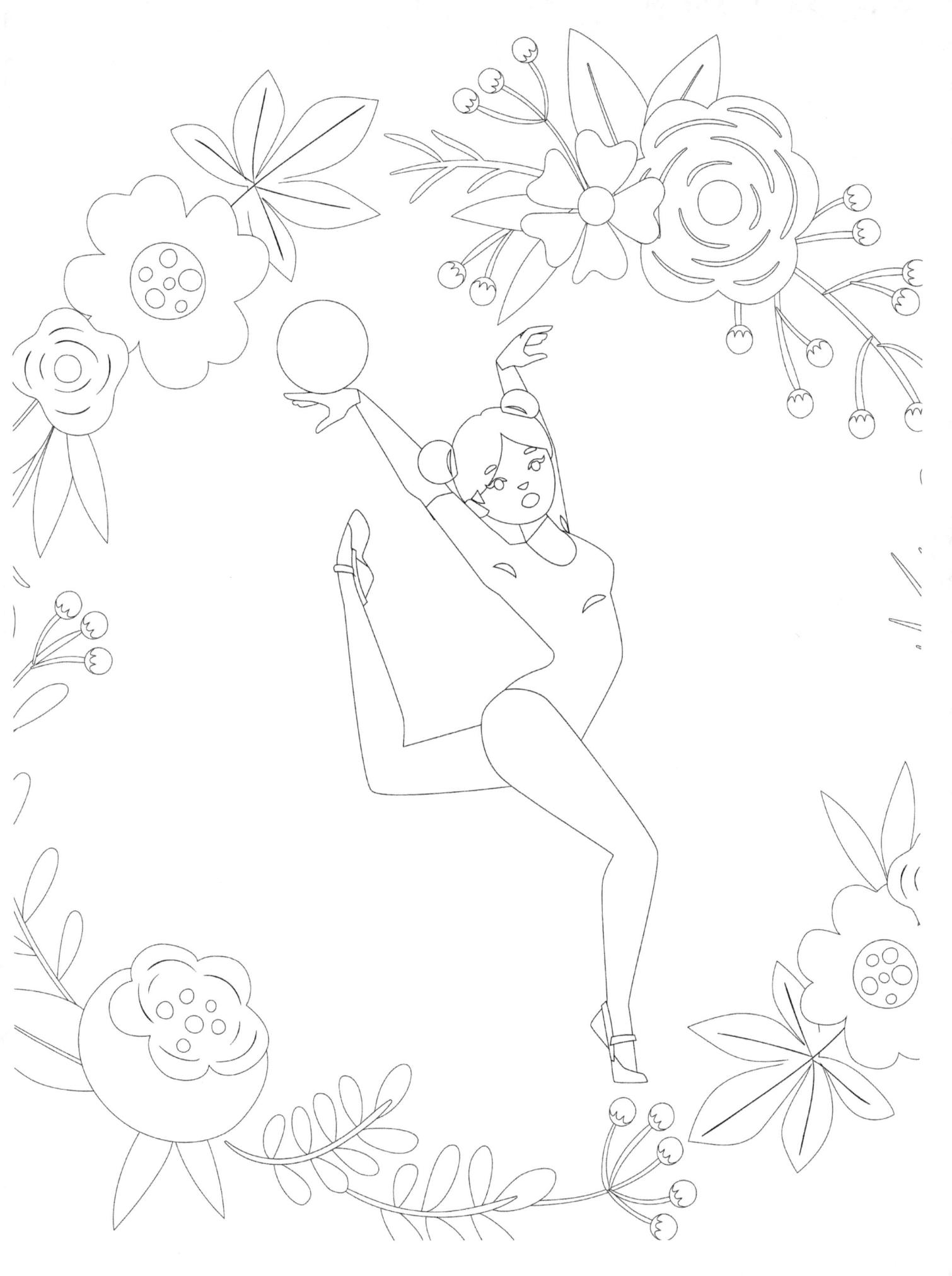

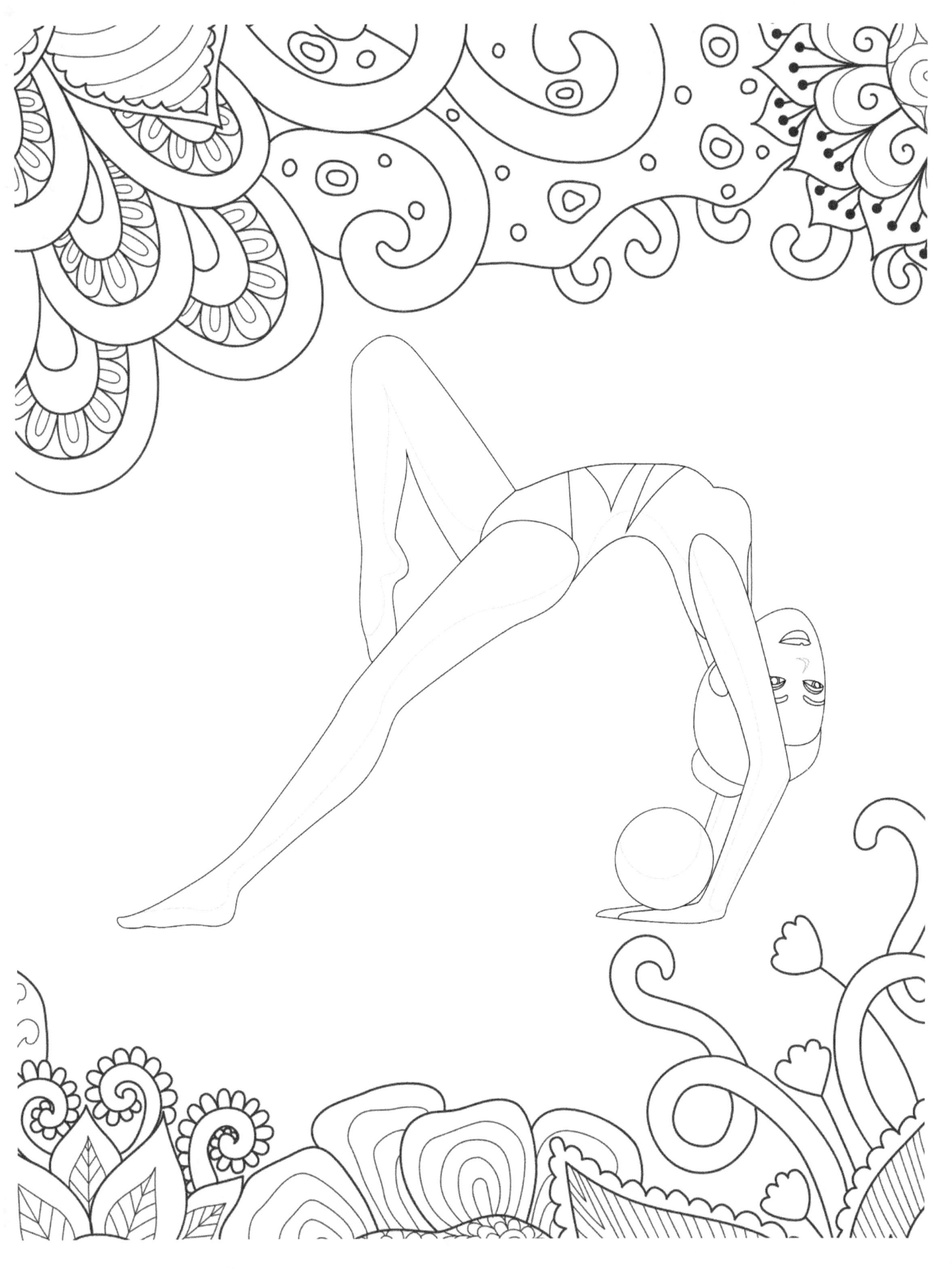

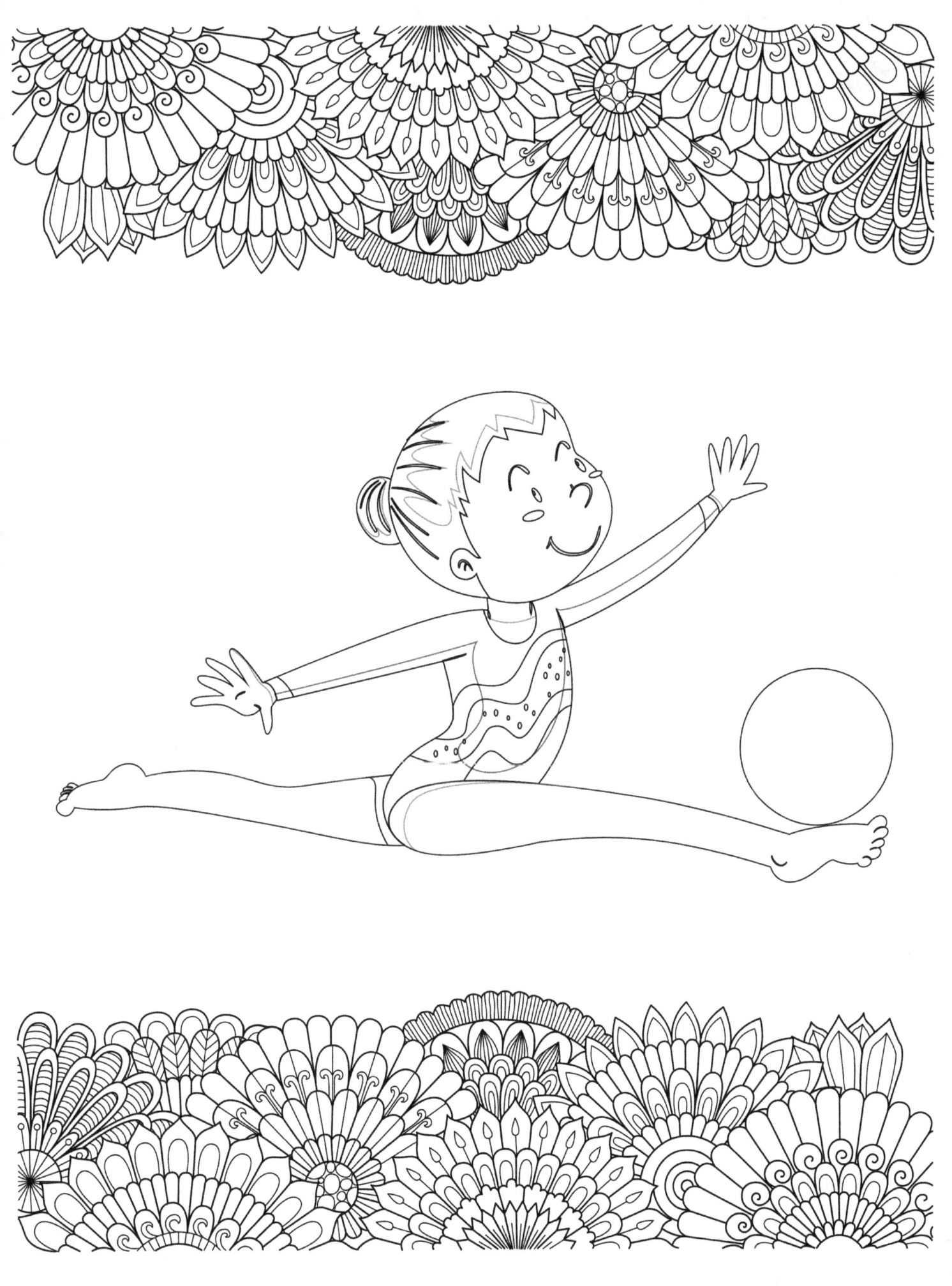

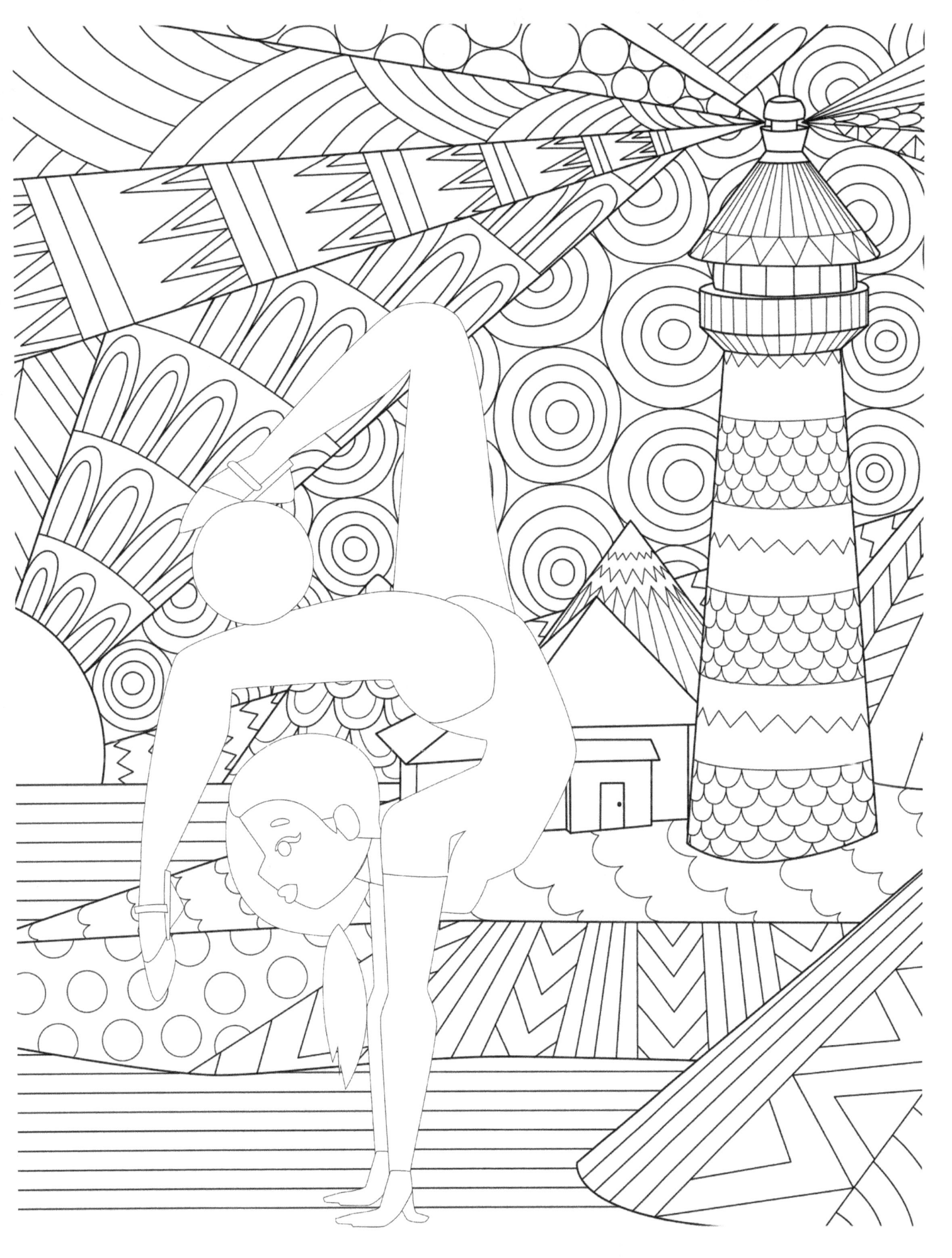

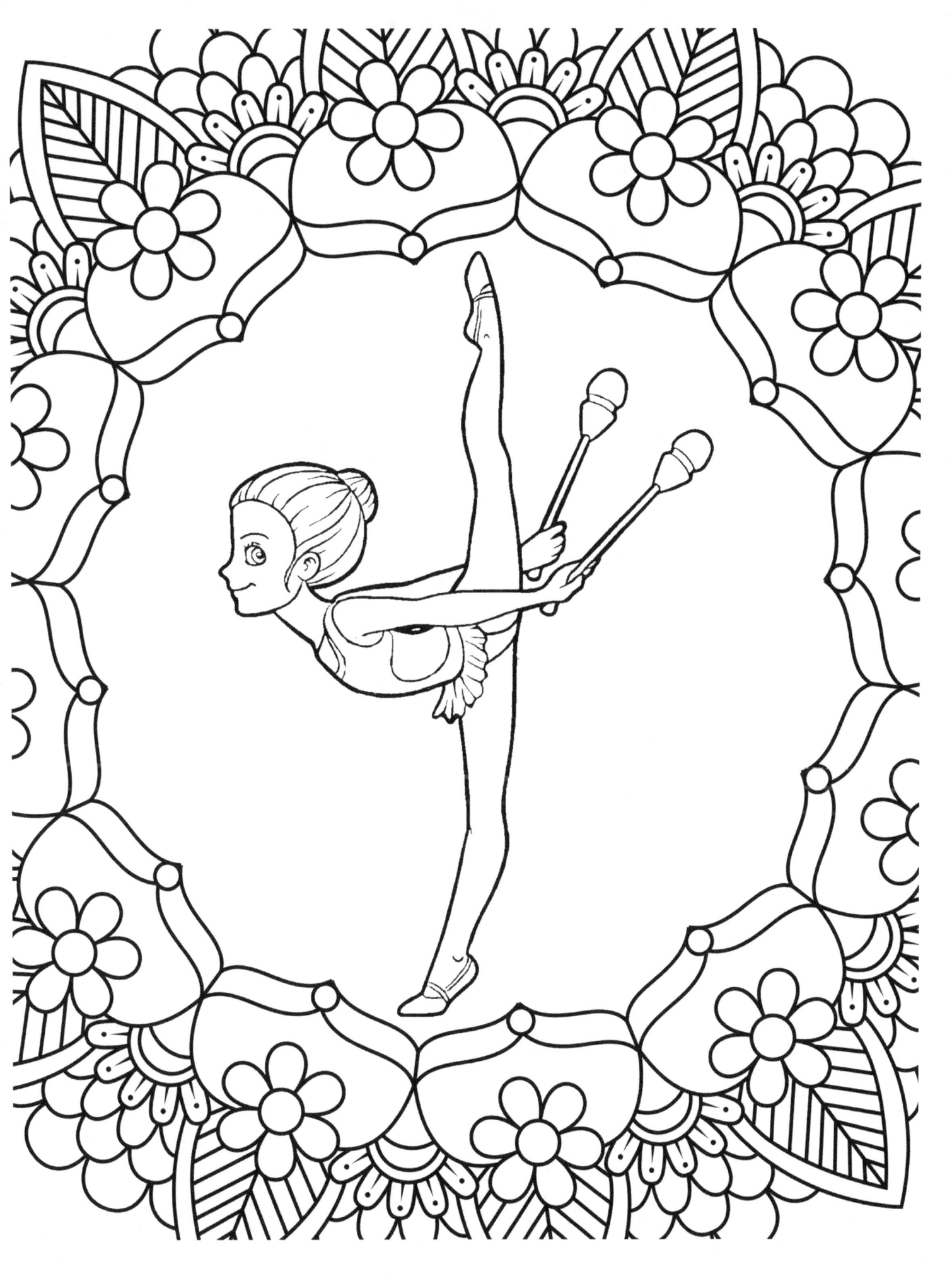

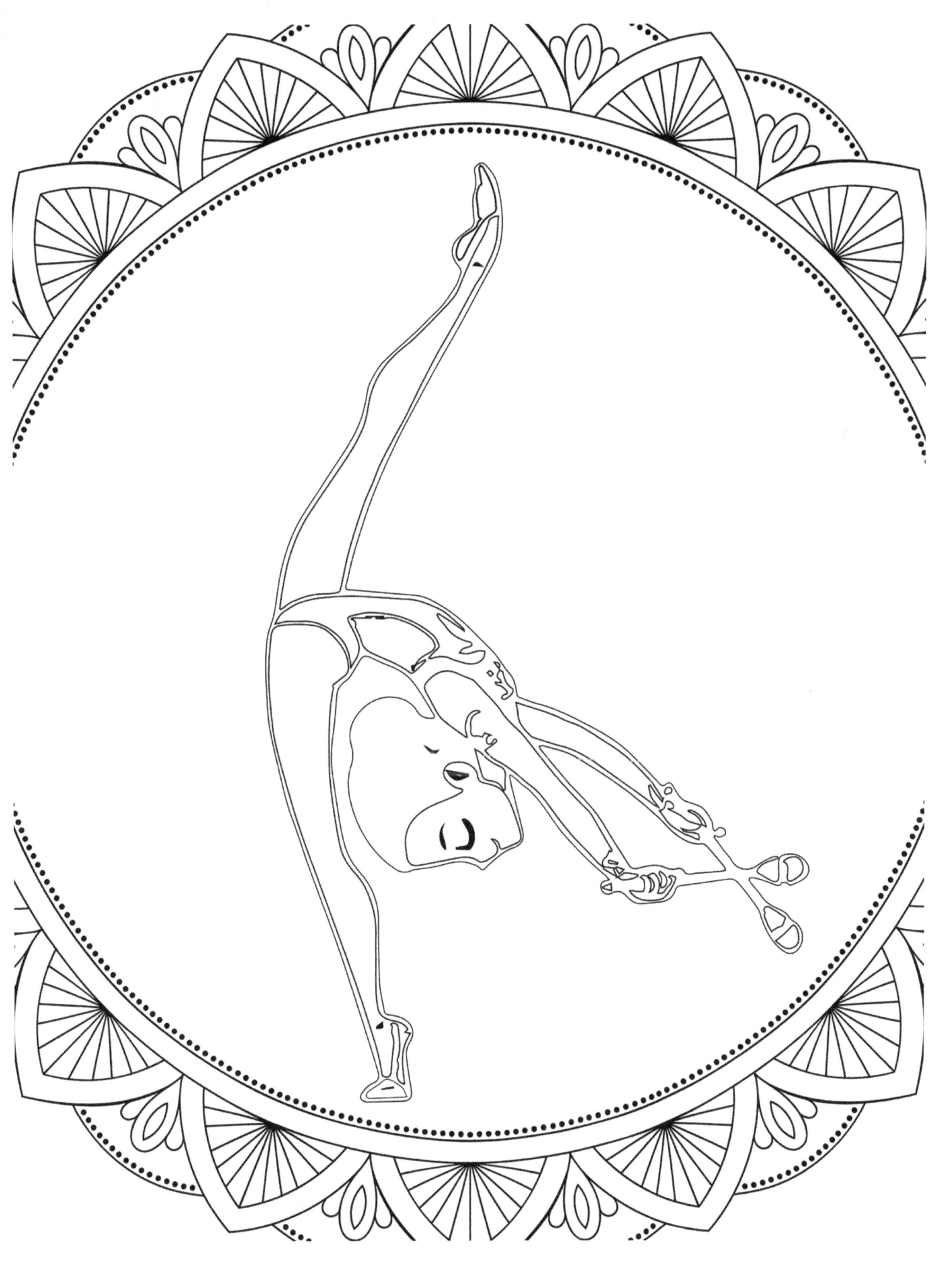

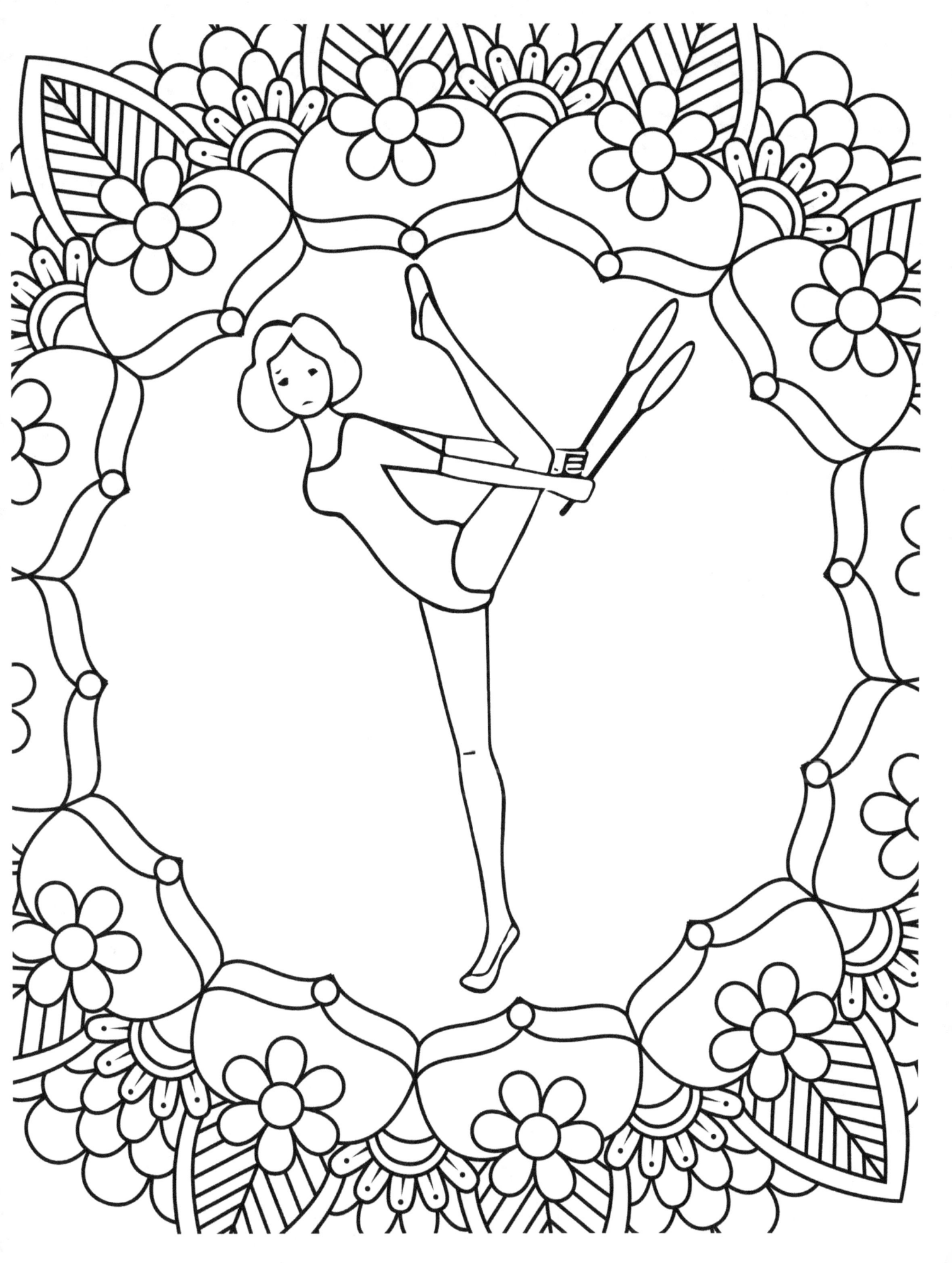

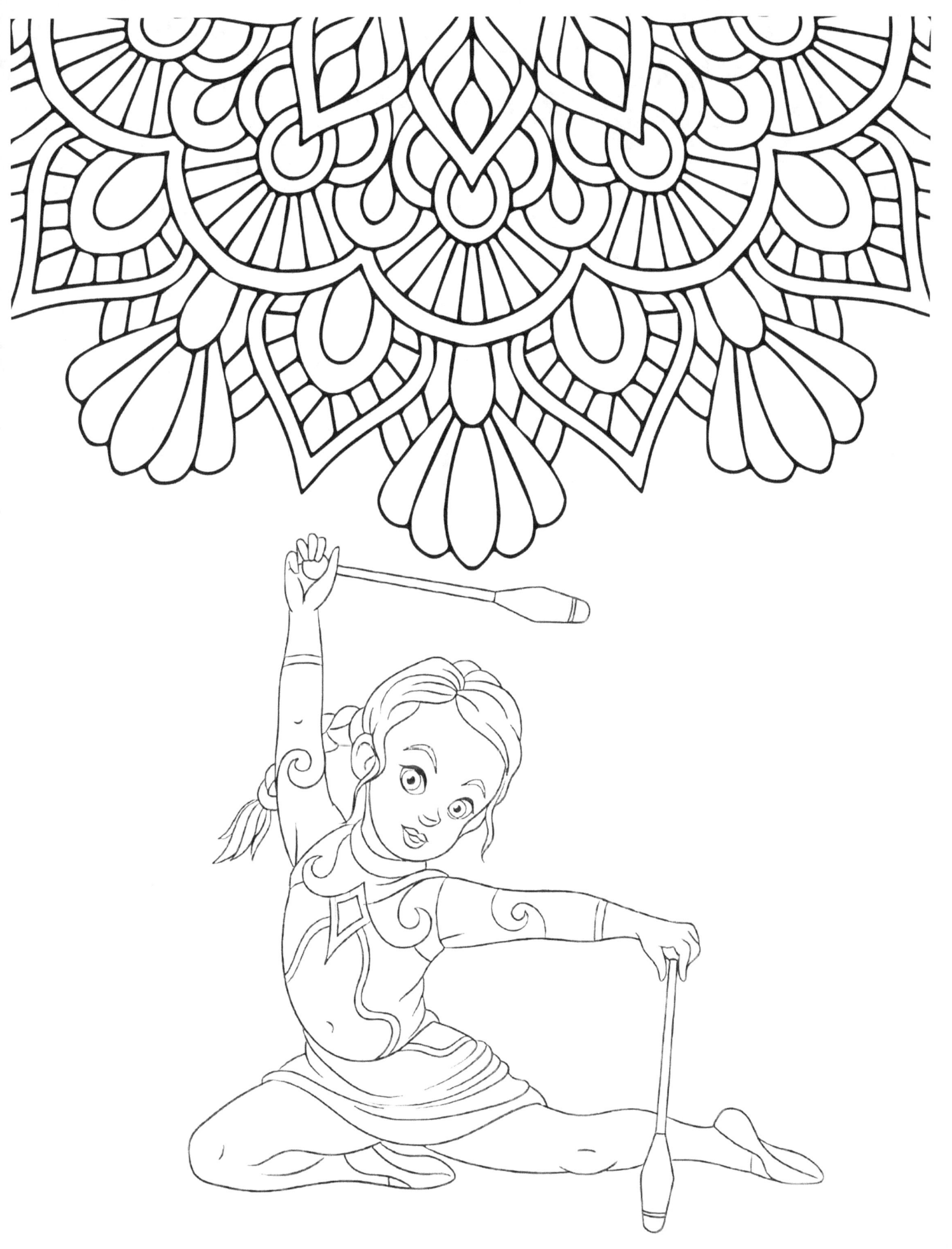

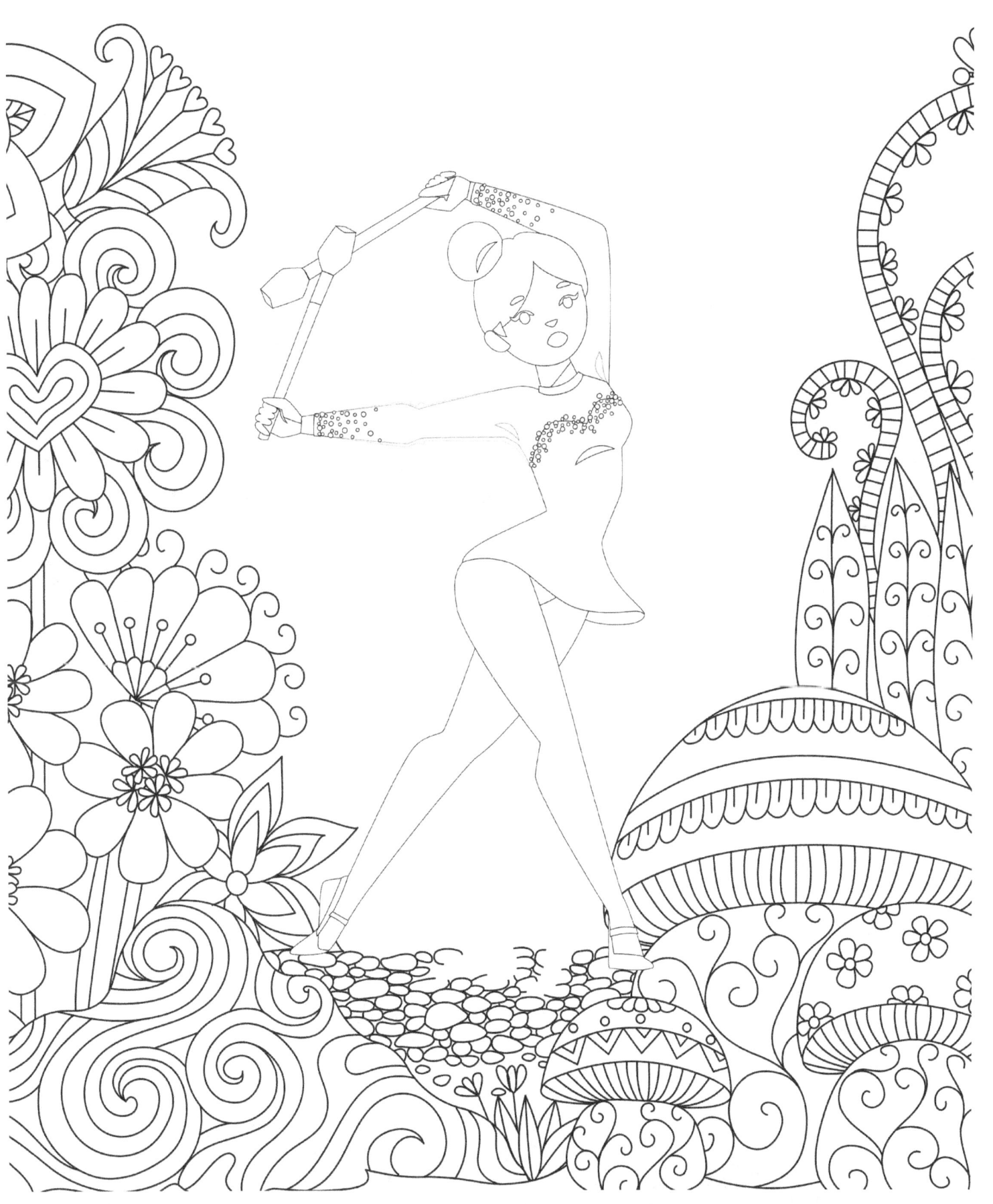

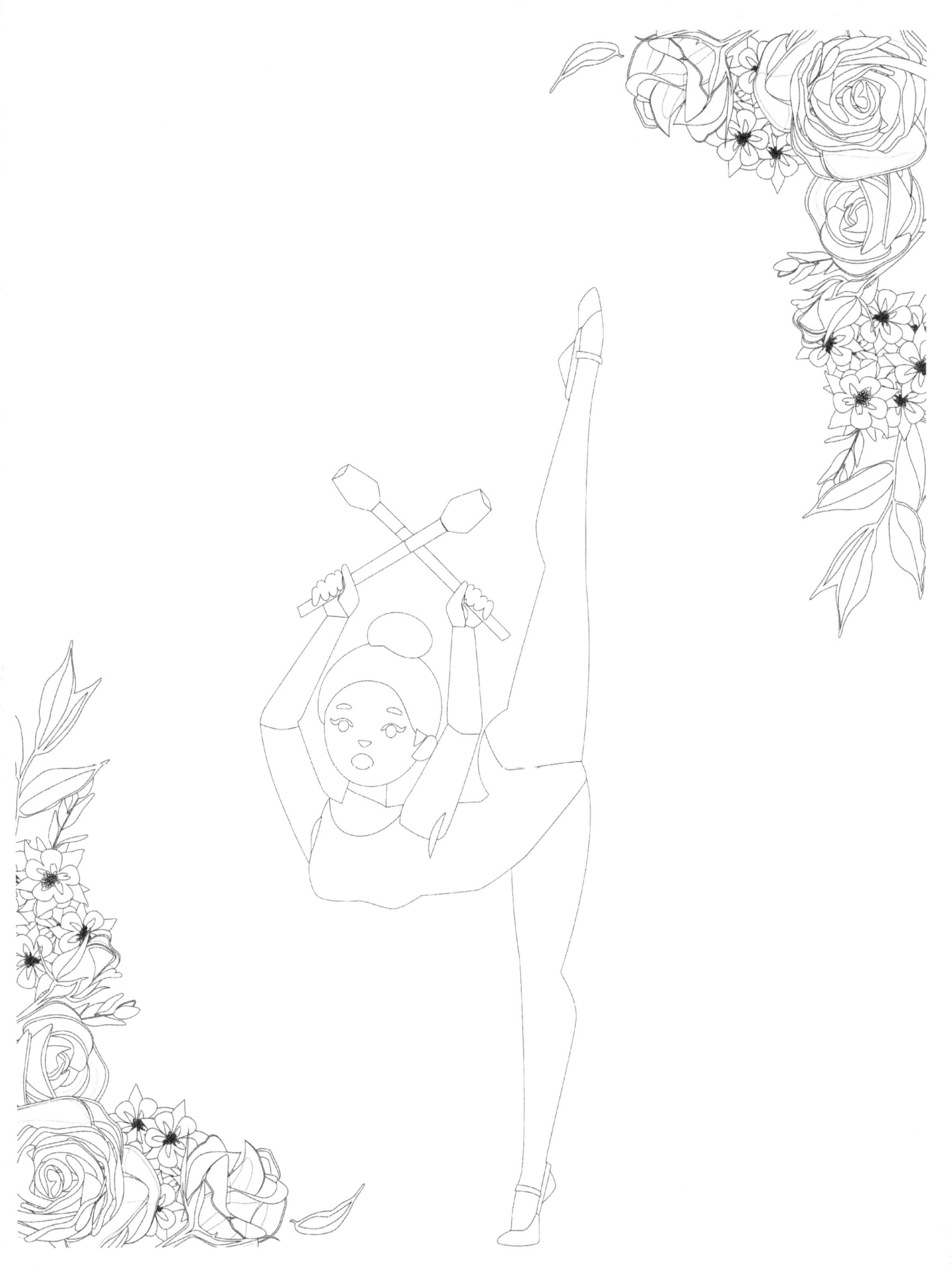

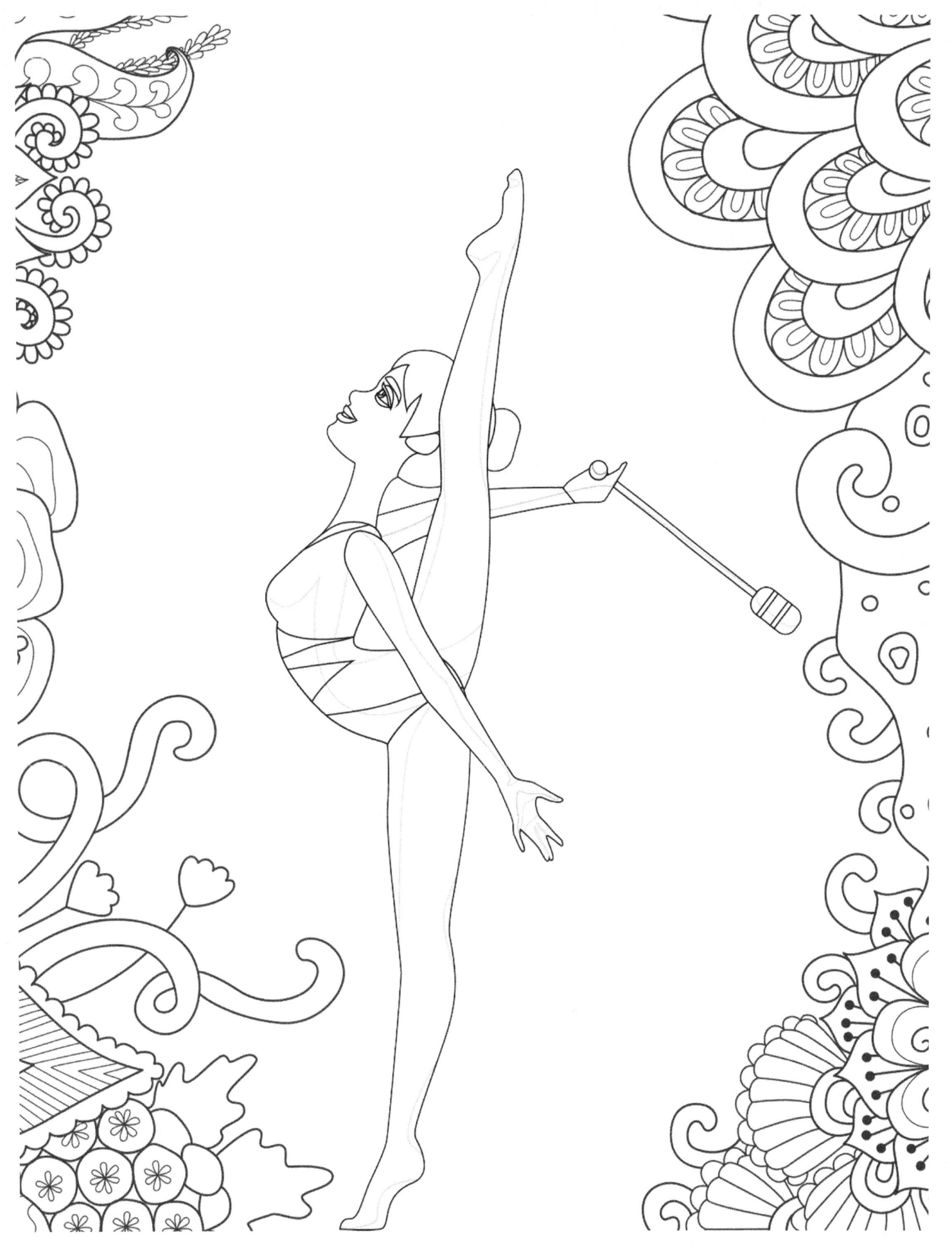

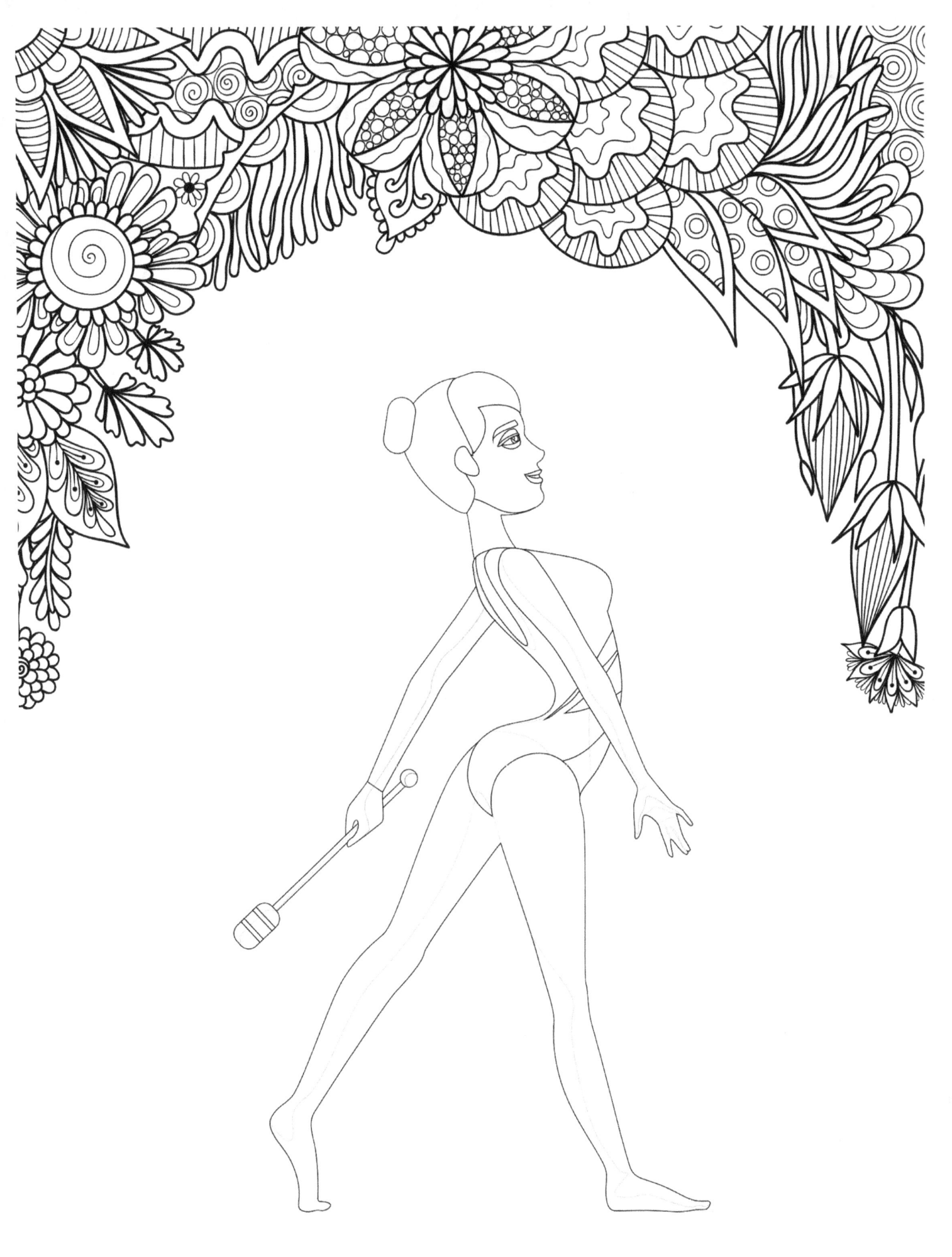

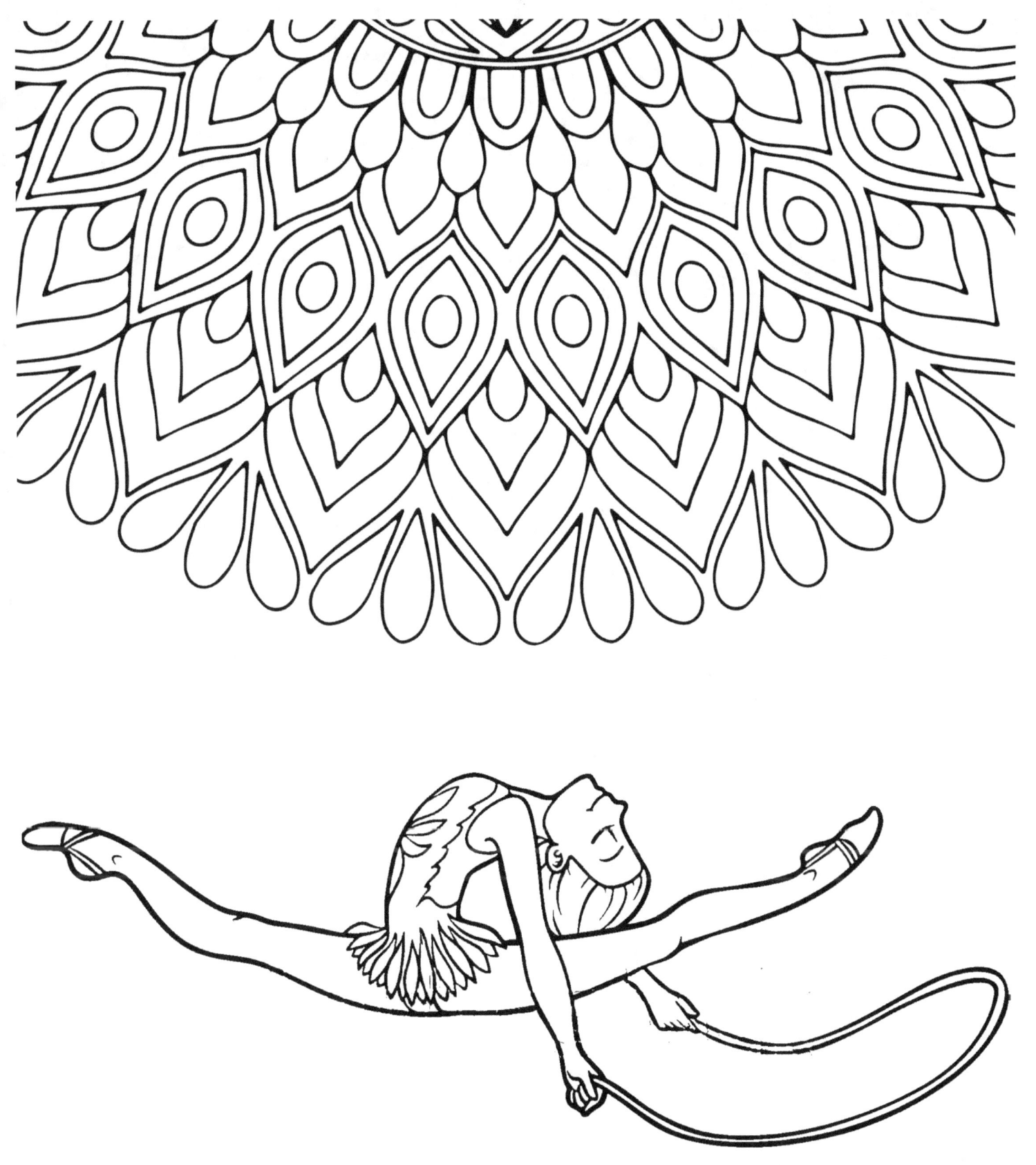

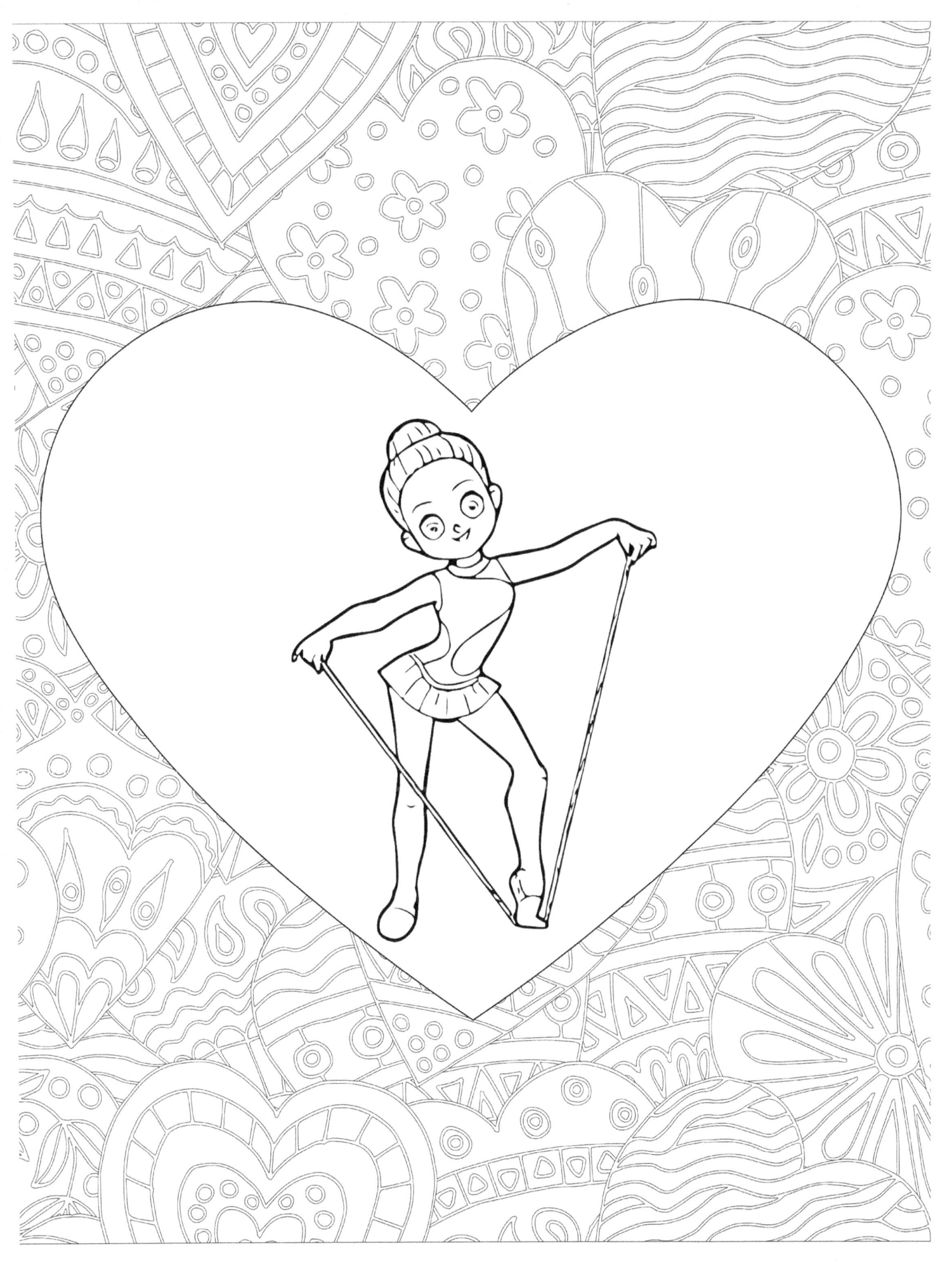

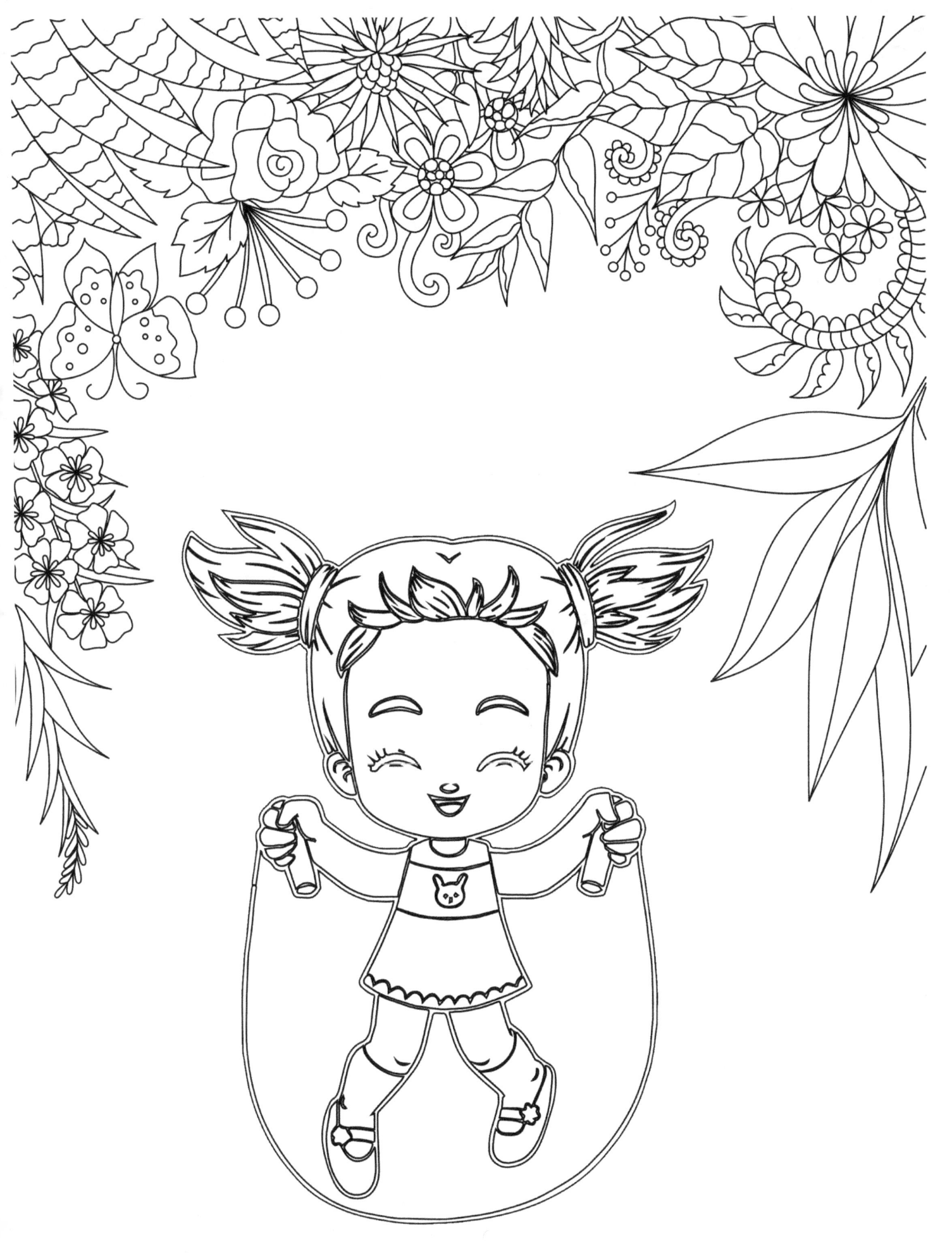

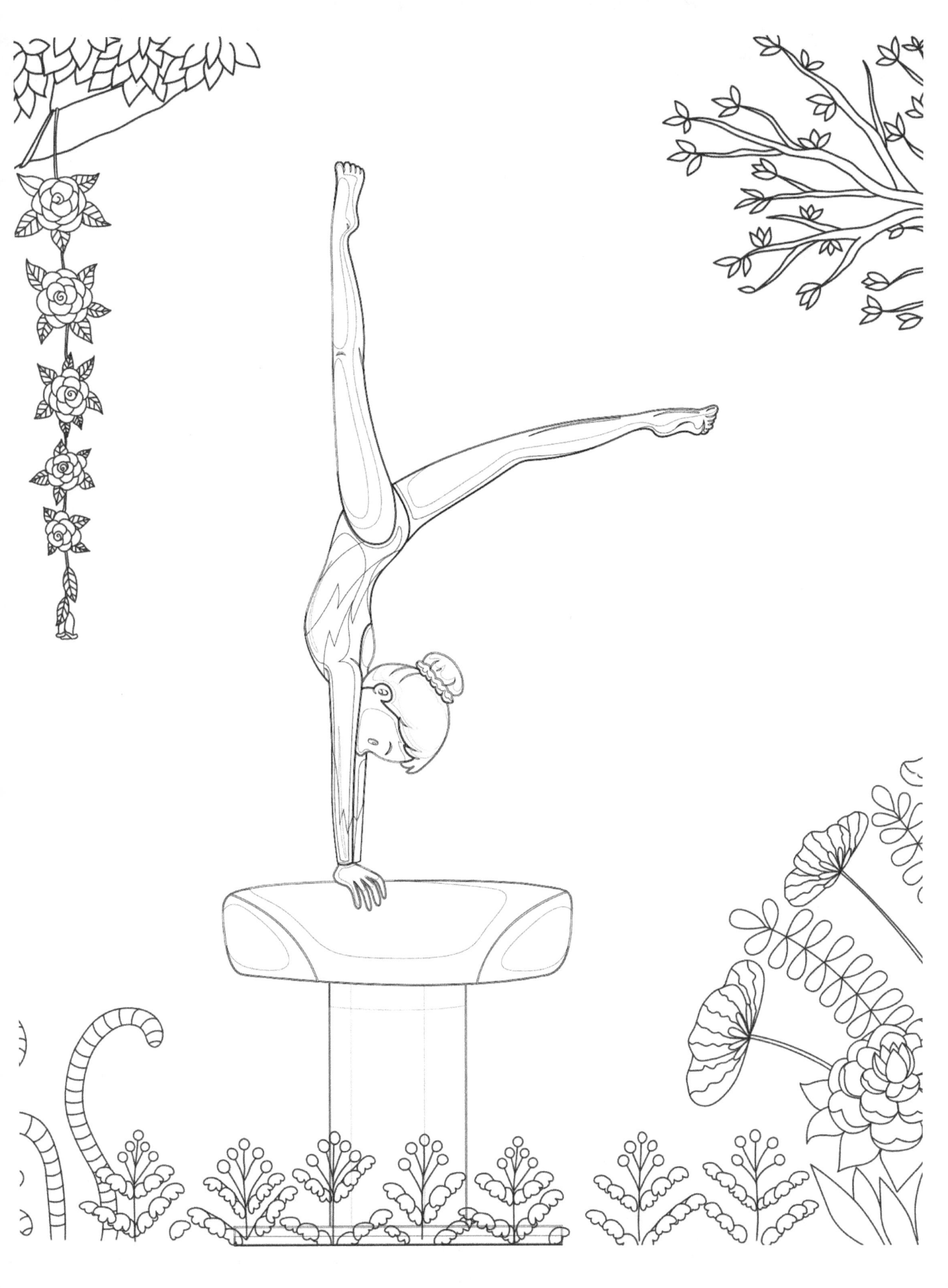

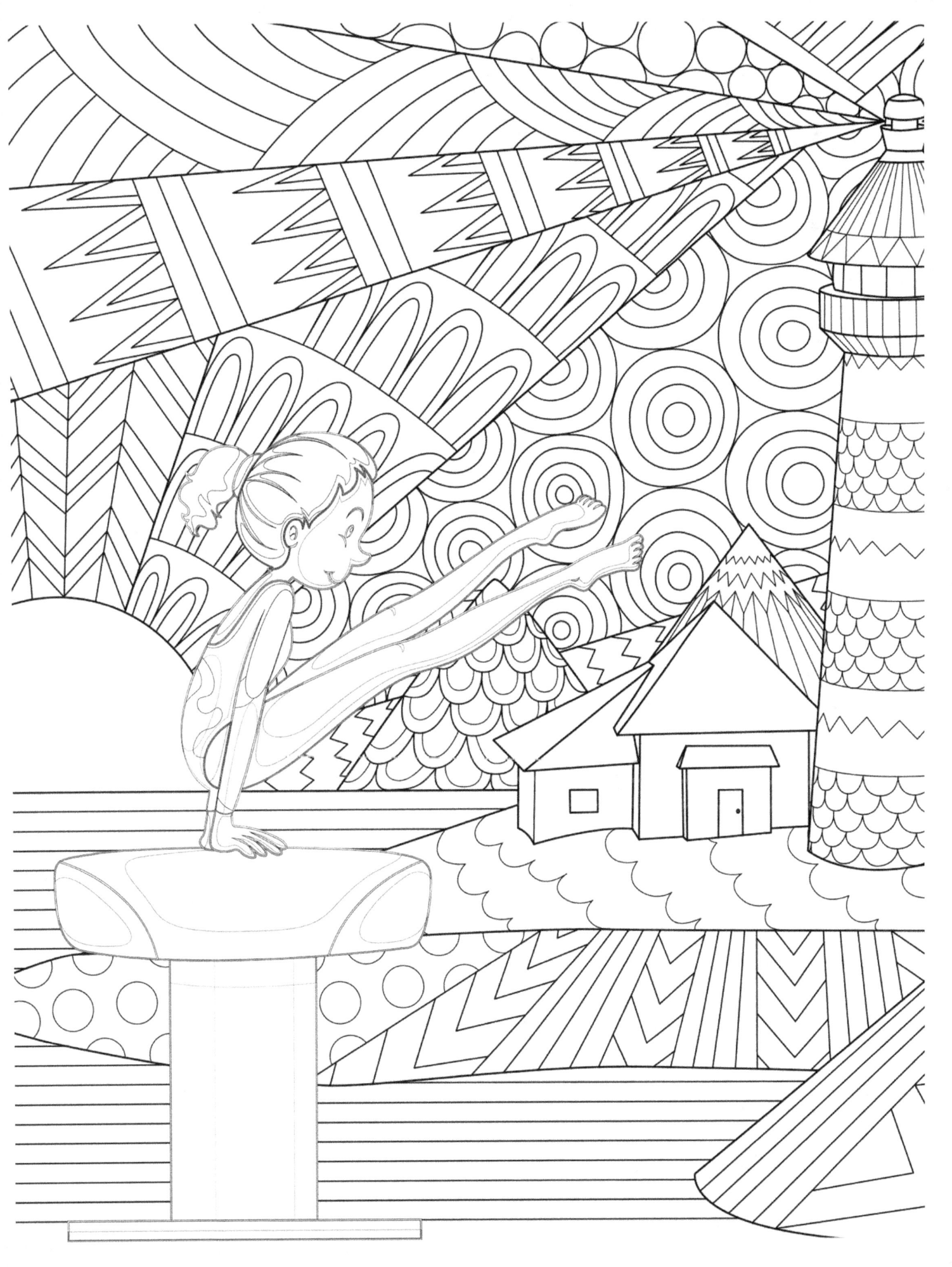

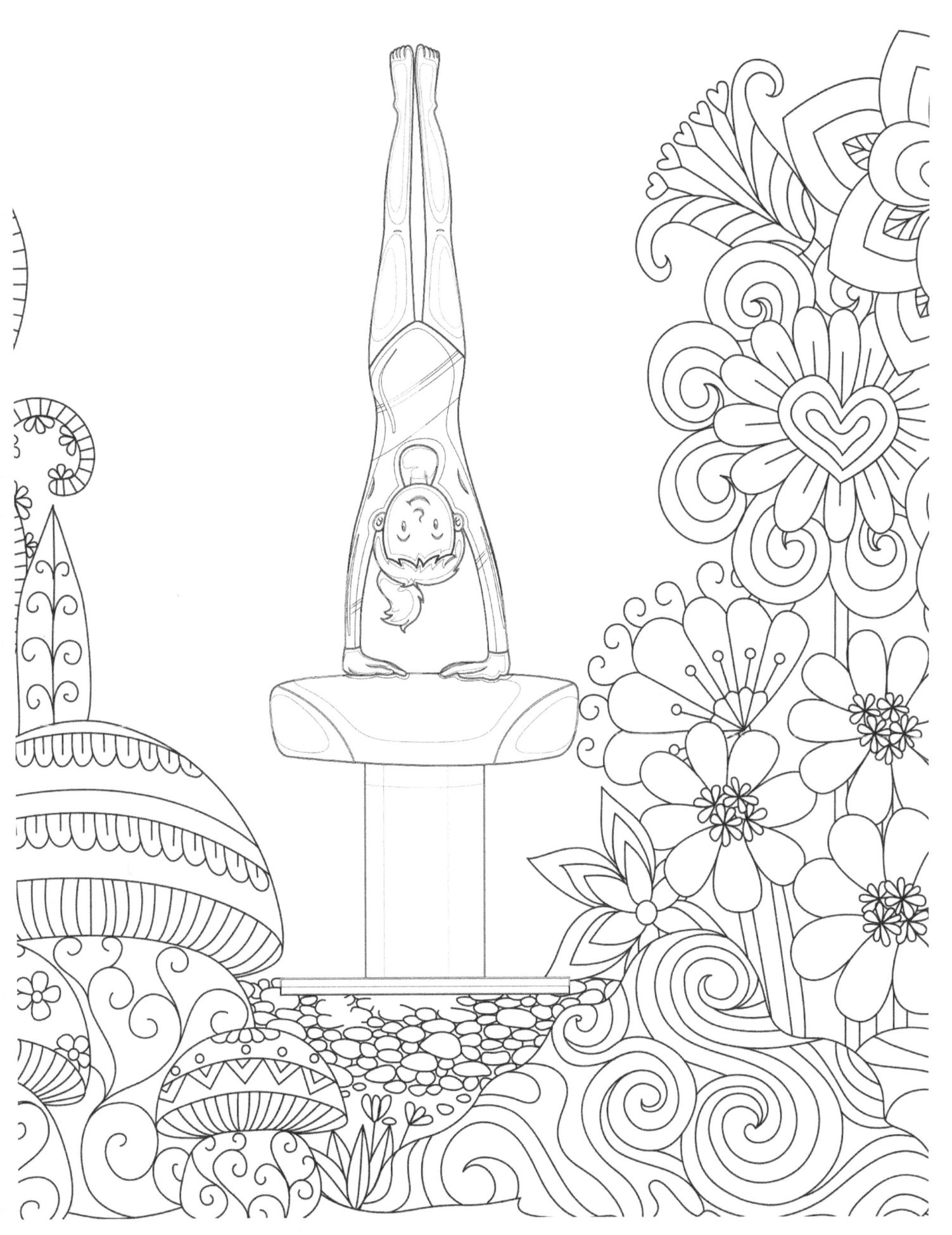

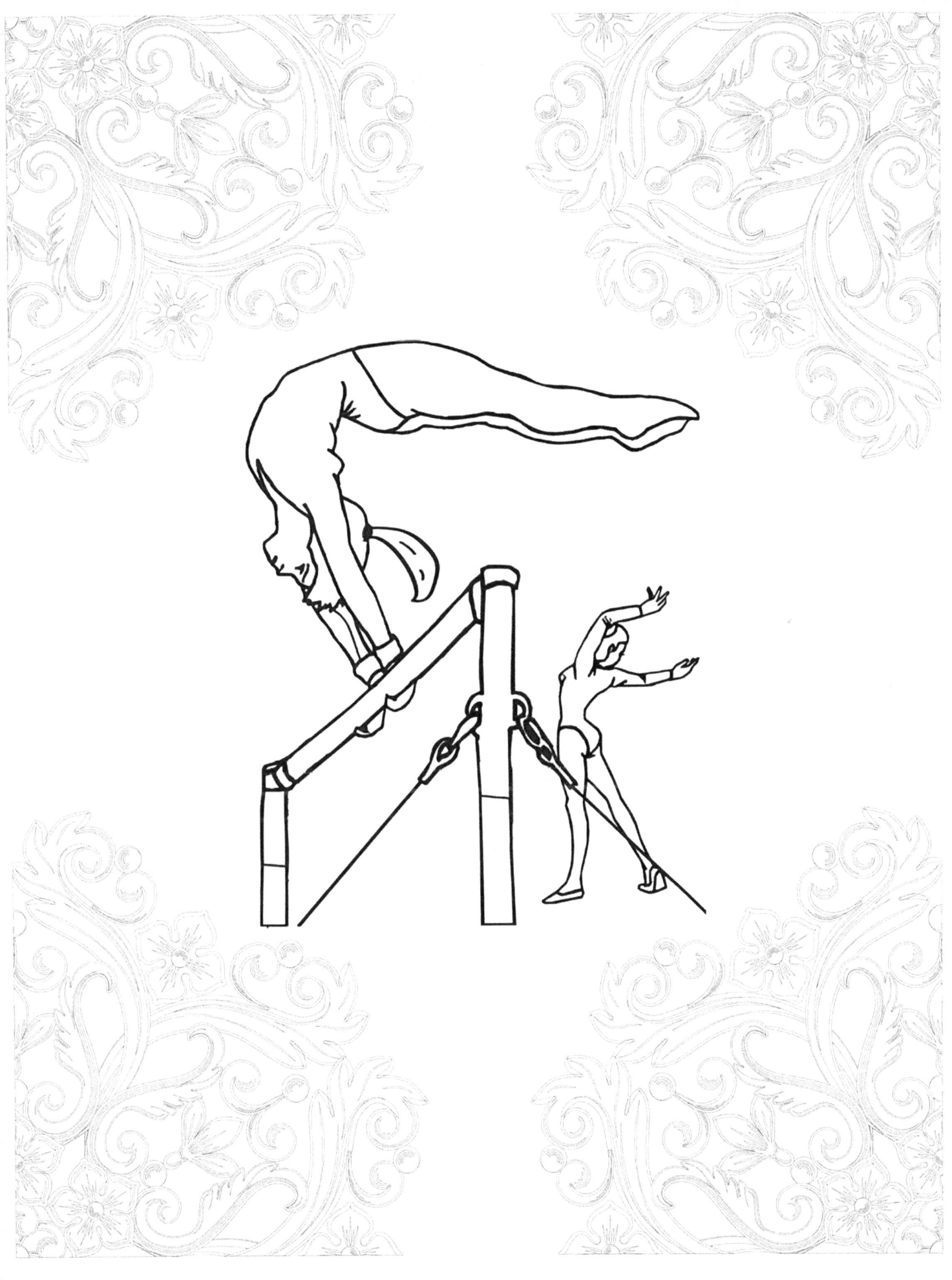

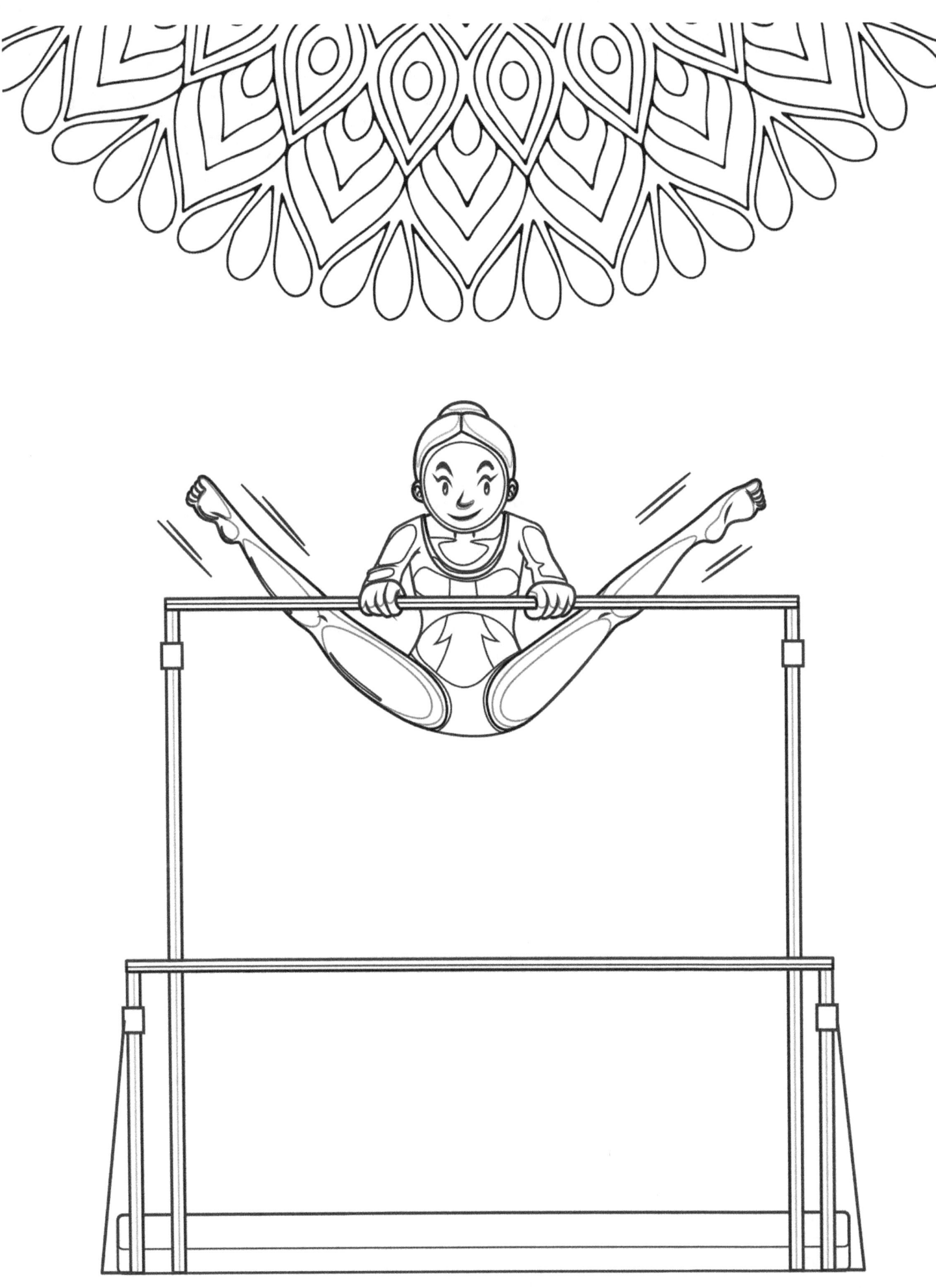

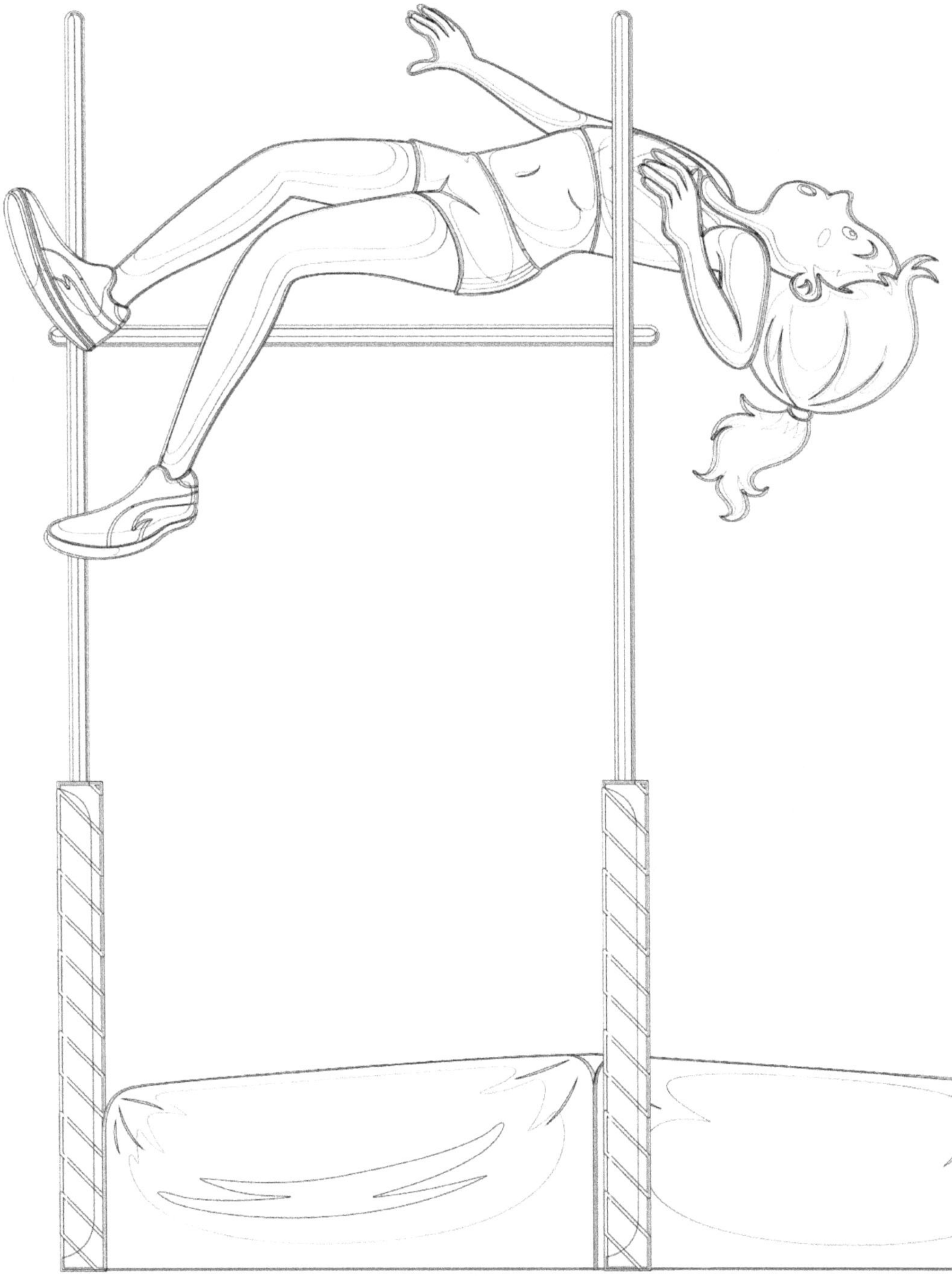

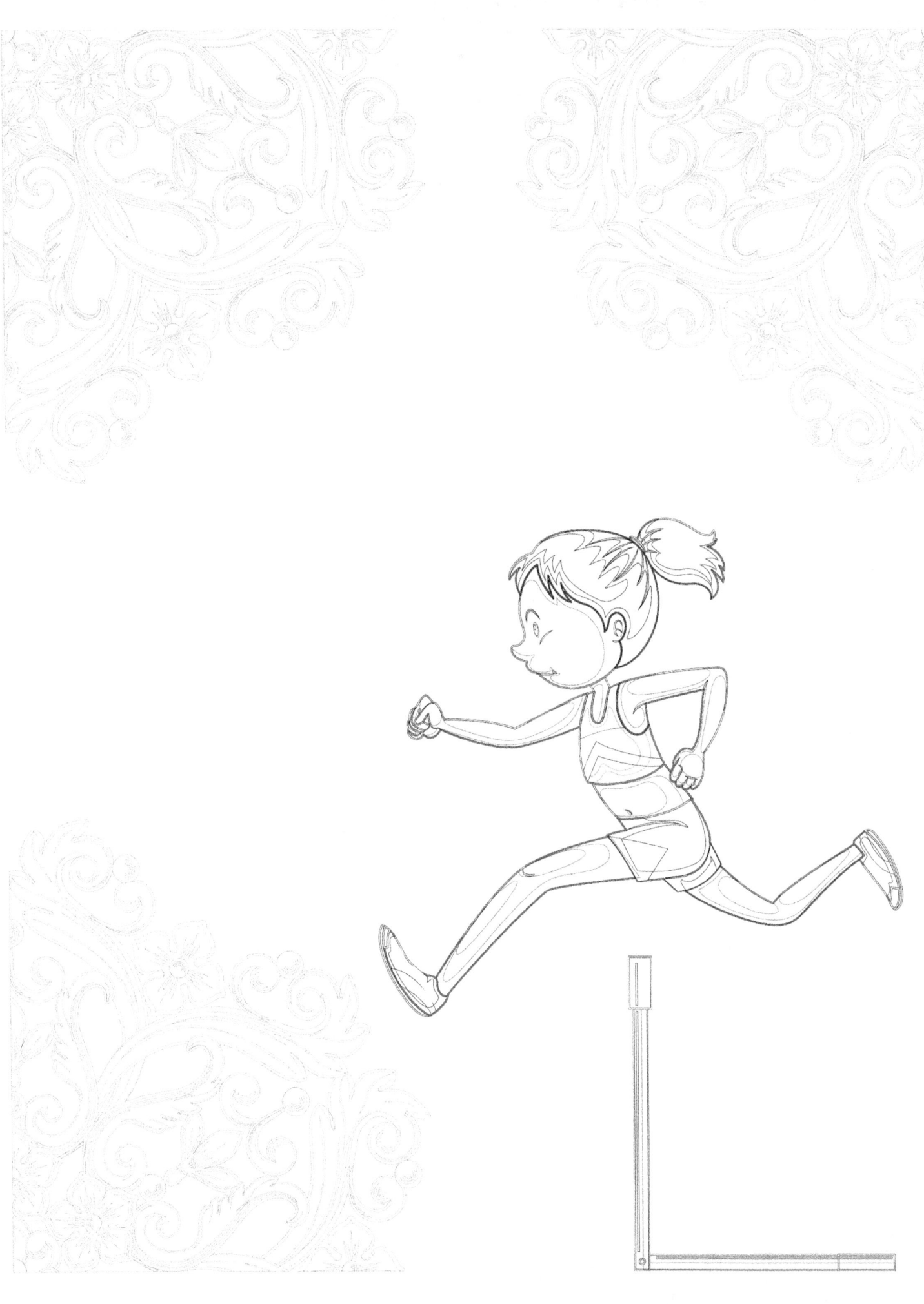

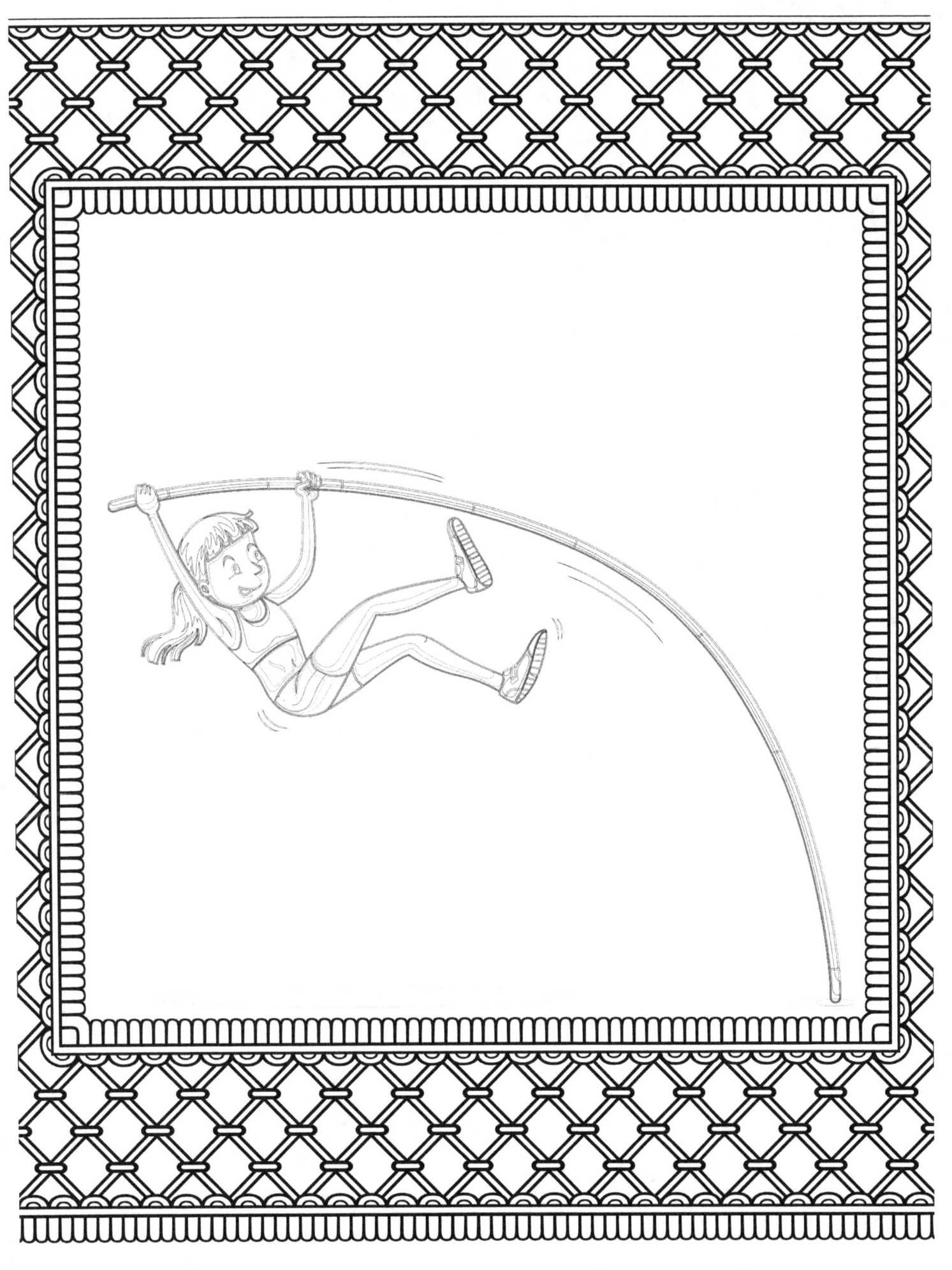

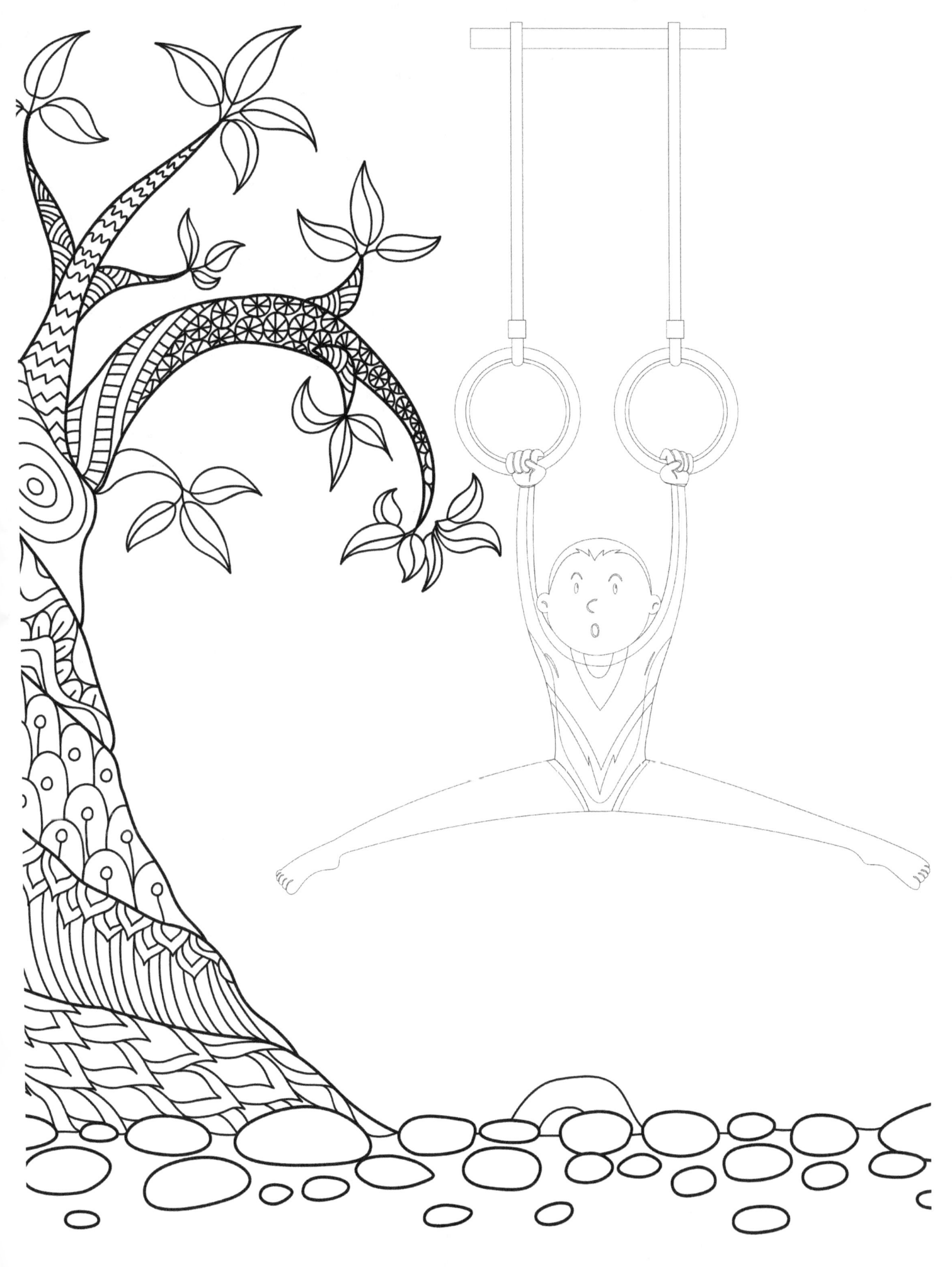

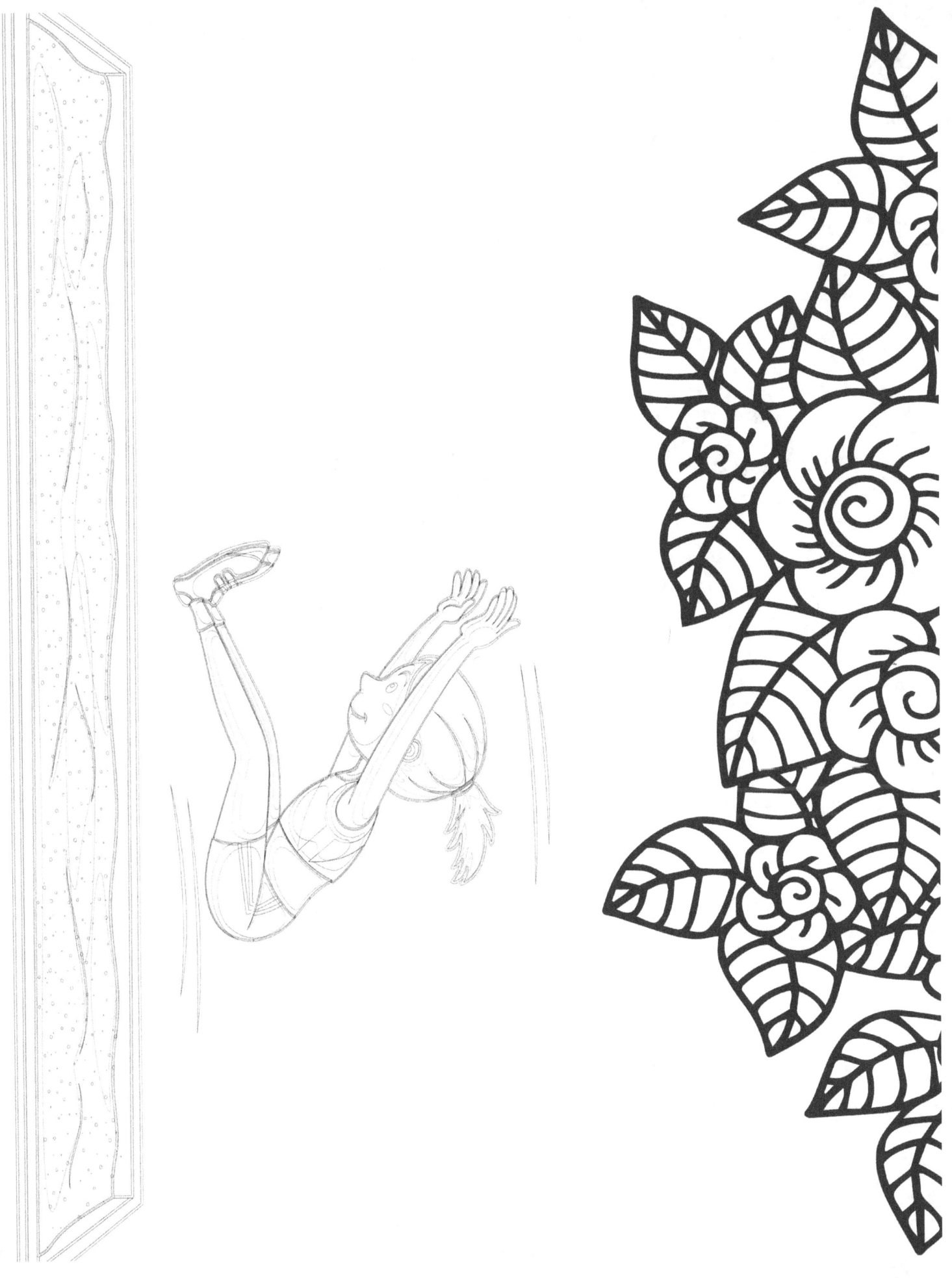

www.ingramcontent.com/pod-product-compliance
Lightning Source LLC
Chambersburg PA
CBHW080511220526
45465CB00006B/2443